S0-BJN-426

About the Author

H. Leo Eddleman has been president of New Orleans Baptist Theological Seminary since 1959. Until assuming that position he served for five years as president of Georgetown (Kentucky) College.

He was pastor of Parkland Baptist Church in Louisville, Kentucky for ten years. He also served as a missionary in Palestine for seven years before war conditions forced him to leave.

Born in Mississippi, Dr. Eddleman is a graduate of Mississippi College and holds the Th.M. and Ph.D. degrees from Southern Baptist Theological Seminary.

Dr. Eddleman has written several books and numerous newspaper and magazine articles.

The Second Coming

The Second Coming

Compiled by *H. Leo Eddlman*

BROADMAN PRESS
Nashville, Tennessee

© 1963 • Broadman Press
All rights reserved

422-217

DEWEY DECIMAL CLASSIFICATION: 232.6
Library of Congress catalog card number: 64-10814
Printed in the United States of America
5.JUL6313

Preface

THE rapid production of thermonuclear devices keeps the subject of "last things" very warm in the nontheological world. While many pulpiteers have abandoned the subject altogether, scientists and philosophers are reflecting awesomely on the possibility of the immanence of the end of this age. Booth Tarkington wrote several years after the atomic bomb fell on Hiroshima, "I am a frightened man."

More pertinent reasons than the recent startling developments in science, however, have stimulated this writer's attention to the subject. Eschatology in general and the second coming in particular have a natural and compelling interest of their own. But more importantly, the "blessed hope" was firmly ensconced in the faith of early Christians. To recapture, or rather to be captured by, the spirit of the first-century Christians, we modern believers should give serious attention to the New Testament emphasis on the second coming. Also, we should take more seriously the lordship of Christ, the Holy Spirit, and the incomparable concept of love which gripped those early disciples. This era witnessed the greatest demonstration of Christianity's spiritual, moral, and social dynamic. Yet during these years Christians erected no church building, held no ecumenical councils. No ecclesiastical organization reached beyond the limits of the city in which it was located if, indeed, it reached that far. No formal institutions were church sponsored. This was the era of faith, hope, and love.

Hope meant the possible immanent return of Christ to this earth. *Eschaton* in Hebrews 1:1 is the Greek origin for our word eschatology or "last thing." The *eschaton* began with the first coming of Christ according to the author of Hebrews. Although it has continued to the present, it has within itself a climactic *eschaton* of its own.

C. H. Dodd startled Christendom some decades ago with his "realized eschatology." Some misconstrued him to say that since the "last thing" had already come, there was nothing more to expect. The rhythmic process of one generation appearing and vanishing only to make way for another would continue indefinitely. This is not fair to C. H. Dodd. If his language appears ambivalent at times, it should be remembered that he leaves room for a visible return of Jesus Christ which is no less a disruption of natural processes than was his first coming.[1]

Some recoil from the New Testament concept of a second coming because it would be so fantastically unlike anything that has ever transpired in human history. Yet the first advent, including the virgin birth and other supernatural phenomena which Christendom has held to even in eras of science and rationalism, was no natural or ordinary phenomenon.

Hermeneutics, or the science of explanation and interpretation, is urgently needed in the study of "last things." If the Bible uses an abundance of figures of speech, imagery, parables, and hyperbole in general, it uses them all the more in connection with the second coming and associated doc-

---

[1]C. H. Dodd, *The Apostolic Preaching* (New York: Harper & Bros., 1936), pp. 82, 85, 90, 93, 96.

trines. One extreme takes the language literally; the other takes it so figuratively as to read out practically all meaning. Somewhere between the two extremes lies the meaning of what the inspired Word is saying.

This does not mean that truth necessarily lies in the middle of anything. It does mean that figurative language challenges the interpreter to discover its intended meaning without trying to read into a given passage more than the figure was intended to convey. When Jesus said, "I am the light of the world," he did not mean that he is composed of electromagnetic waves rushing through space at the rate of 186,300 miles per second. He did mean that as "the light of the world" he dispels the darkness of ignorance, iniquity, and even fear itself. To get behind the symbol to the actual meaning is the task of the interpreter.

To subject such aspects of the scriptural revelation to the scrutiny of philosophy, science, historical perspective, psychology, and comparable disciplines is a necessary part of the interpreter's task. Yet, the biblical account of the first coming of Christ, much less his second coming, can never be demonstrated conclusively by the formulas of science and mathematics. It is strictly a question of faith regarding the Christian revelation. Revelational truth cannot be demonstrated empirically, although there may be more scientific and philosophical evidence for it than there is for the conclusions of the fluid science of some contemporary psychology.

It is not the purpose of the compiler to try to make the subject at hand congenial to the modern mind, palatable to the cynical spirit, or intellectually acceptable to the pure rationalist. Divine wisdom has seen fit to project all revelation recorded in the Scriptures within a framework of "divine incognito." There is a certain subjectivism about all faith and Christian experience which, while conclusive to the scien-

tifically minded believer, cannot be proved by him to another.

The viewpoints expressed in this symposium are those of
the individual authors and have no relationship to any official
statement on the second coming by the institution, the profes-
sors, or the denomination which the compiler serves. Each
contributor is responsible for the interpretations in his chapter. Dedicated scholars throughout Christendom hold to
different positions on the subject. This augments rather than
nullifies the need for continued dialogue.

Dr. J. D. Grey, pastor of the First Baptist Church, New
Orleans, Louisiana, had actually begun a similar compilation
some four years ago, and the present writer was one of his
contributors. However, it was decided for several reasons to
get the volume before the public in the present manner. The
mutual concern was, more than anything else, the desire to
precipitate more interest in him whose lordship supplied the
spiritual, moral, and social dynamic for early Christians.

H. LEO EDDLEMAN

Contents

ix

1
Jesus Is Coming to Earth Again

ANGEL MARTINEZ

THE second coming of Jesus Christ is the hope of the church and the solution to human history. We know that he came the first time, and that is a matter of history. We know that he shall come again, and that is a matter of prophecy. Jesus came the first time to save the soul; he shall come again to save the body. He came the first time to save the individual; he shall come the second time to save society. Christ came the first time to a crucifixion; he shall come the second time to a coronation. He came the first time to a tree; he shall come the second time to a throne. The first time that Jesus came, he stood before Pilate; the next time that he comes, Pilate shall stand before him.

The second coming of our Lord is a must because of the helplessness of man. Man is a dependent creature; his achievements are synthetic, not creative. Jesus Christ came the first time because man was not able to redeem himself. The human race has made efforts at self-redemption. Adam and Eve began the attempt in the Garden of Eden when they sewed the fig leaves. From that day until the present hour man has been feverishly trying to extricate himself from the quicksand of human depravity. The course of history reveals his failure. Good deeds, charitable generosity, ethical dealings have not been a solution. As good as they are on the human level, they fail to meet the perfect standards of a holy God.

Thus the cross became the answer to man's inability to save himself. Salvation must be a work of grace in its totality. The cross reveals God at his best; it reveals man at his worst. Before Jesus died on the cross, men would go to a cross to die. This was the method of execution for criminals, analogous to our electric chair or gas chamber. Since Jesus died on the cross, men now go to the cross to live. The seat of death has become the source of life. This is God's answer to man's helplessness on the individual level.

Not only is man individually helpless, thereby needing divine intervention—the crucifixion—in order to procure his salvation. There is another area of his dependence: man is socially helpless. Peruse the pages of history and you will find this to be true. Wars and rumors of wars, nation rising against nation and kingdom rising against kingdom, race hatreds, class hatreds, political hatreds, economical hatreds—all prove that man intensifies his problem in the attempt to solve it. We are experts at winning wars, but we are also experts in losing the peace. Science has made the world a neighborhood but not a brotherhood. One can board a jet airplane and be anywhere in the world in a few hours. Technical progress has drawn the world closer geographically but not spiritually.

What is the solution? God must intervene again. The Word of God teaches that Christ must come again. Then every knee shall bow before him and every tongue shall confess that he is Lord to the glory of God the Father (Rom. 14:11). The spear shall be turned into a pruning hook and the sword shall be beaten into a plowshare (Isa. 2:4). The lamb and the wolf shall feed together (Isa. 65:25), and the knowledge of God shall cover the earth as the waters cover the sea (Isa. 11:9). This is the answer to man's blunders and defeats. There is no other solution to the human situation. No wonder the closing verse in the Bible is a prayer for our Lord's return, "Even so, come, Lord Jesus."

In the first chapter of the book of Habakkuk, the prophet is lamenting because of the horrible conditions that prevail in his country. Spoiling and violence are everywhere; strife and contention abound in the land. The law is slacked, and judgment is not just. The good man loses and the bad man wins. In the light of these conditions, the prophet asks God for a solution. In Habakkuk 1:5 we find these words: "Behold ye among the heathen, and regard, and wonder marvellously: for I will work a work in your days, which ye will not believe, though it be told you." This verse is quoted in Acts 13:41 in connection with the statement that through Jesus men would receive the remission of sins. So God is saying to Habakkuk: I will take care of the conditions that prevail around you through the crucifixion; I will send a Redeemer.

Then Habakkuk states: "Thou art of purer eyes than to behold evil, and canst not look on iniquity: wherefore lookest thou upon them that deal treacherously, and holdest thy tongue when the wicked devoureth the man that is more righteous than he?" (1:13). In other words, the prophet is saying: Lord, I can understand how I can look on evil, for I am corrupt; but how do you stand it? You are pure and holy. How can you put up with it; how will you solve it for yourself? The prophet continues to describe the lurid conditions that prevail and his amazement that God can stand the sight. When he concludes his tirade against the status quo, he waits for an answer with a trembling heart.

Thus, chapter 2 opens by saying: "I will stand upon my watch, and set me upon the tower, and will watch to see what he will say unto me, and what I shall answer when I am reproved." Let us not forget that this verse should be quoted with a quaver in the voice. Habakkuk is afraid. But the Lord is always reasonable, and in verses 2-4 we have these words:

The Lord answered me, and said, Write the vision, and make it plain upon tables, that he may run that readeth it. For the vision is yet for an appointed time, but at the end it shall speak, and not lie: though it tarry, wait for it; because it will surely come, it will not tarry. . . . but the just shall live by his faith.

In Hebrews 10:37-38 we read, "For yet a little while, and he that shall come will come, and will not tarry. Now the just shall live by faith." In other words, when the prophet asked: "O Lord, why do I have to look on this corruption; what will you do about it?" God answered, "I will put my son on a cross." When the prophet asked how God could look on it, the Lord replied, "I will send my son again." The second coming is the answer to the evil of the day. Jesus will not tarry; he will surely come.

In the Old Testament, the rabbis were often confused by the seeming contradictions in the descriptions of the coming of the Messiah. In some of the passages the Messiah was described as coming as a Suffering Servant to be wounded for transgressions and bruised for iniquities. In other passages he was coming as a conqueror to rule and to defeat the enemies of the people of God. The people asked their scholars for an answer to this seeming contradiction. The rabbis often would go so far as to say that two Messiahs were coming. They were wrong; the same Messiah was coming twice.

With an average of one verse to every twenty-five, the New Testament speaks of this glorious return of Christ. Thus, in the New Testament the doctrine of the second coming receives frequent mention. Why did the Holy Spirit prompt that he came, he came to redeem; the next time that he comes, he shall come to reign. The first time that he came, he came as a servant; the next time that he comes, he shall come as a sovereign. The first time that he came, he was refused a drink; the next time he comes, grateful believers will procure the best drink that earth can produce.

One day Jesus took a short trip in a boat with his disciples. The waters were calm and the winds blew gently. But presently, the climate changed. The lake became rough, and the gentle winds became enraged and turned into a cruel gale. The lightning began to play in the pavilion of the cloud. The thunder began to roll and the fragile ship began to swing and sway and creak and crack, and the disciples paled and looked at one another and said, "Tonight we die." Jesus was sleeping placidly at one end of the boat. The disciples aroused Jesus from his sleep and said, "Carest thou not that we perish?" (Mark 4:38). Jesus arose and before he rebuked the storm, he rebuked the disciples, saying, "O ye of little faith" (Matt. 8:26). Then he calmed the feverish storm; the waves ceased their fury. The winds became calm, the clouds dispersed, the yellow light of the moon came through again.

This is a parable of what will happen when Christ returns. We are living in turbulent days. The ship of civilization has encountered a storm. Wars are blooming in the field of human discord. Borders are bristling with bayonets. Men's hearts are failing them for fear. Hatreds, individual and international, are incubating in the bosom of humanity. The spiritual barometer is dropping rapidly. Even though church membership is at an all-time high, morals are at an all-time low. Homes are breaking up; faithfulness in marriage is going with the wind. It seems as if the world will not come out of this catastrophe. But Christ will come again, and he will speak in kindred language, "Peace be still." And when he does, every cannon will be muzzled, every gun will be spiked.

Every submarine and airplane will say, "Let me be the
servant of man, and not his destroyer." Even so, come, Lord
Jesus.

The church cannot produce the victory that Christ will
bring with him, for everyone will not adhere to the church.
The church struggles with its own imperfections and di-
visions. We were given a graphic picture of this when Christ
was on the mount of transfiguration. While the disciples
waited for him to return, a distraught father enjoined the
followers of Jesus to heal his little boy. The disciples tried
and prayed and did all that they knew but to no avail. When
Christ came down from the mountain, the father rushed to
him and said: "I brought him to your disciples, and they could
not heal him. Lord, help me." Jesus healed the boy instantly,
and the disciples were confused. Why couldn't they do it?
Their imperfect devotion was the cause.

Christ is in a glorified state today. Here at the bottom of the
hill the church attempts to cast out the devil and heal a sick
civilization. But we are powerless and helpless, even as the
disciples were. One day the Great Physician will descend, and
he will bring healing in his wings. What the church could not
do with its lack of spiritual devotion, Christ will do with the
glory of his coming. This fact does not lessen our responsibility to a lost and sin-sick world, but it makes us keenly
aware of the fact that the body of Christ on earth is not
complete. Christ, the head of the church, will come again,
and that will be glory for the church and peace for the world.

In the book of Matthew, Christ likens his coming to the
lightning that flashes in the sky. He said: "As the lightning
cometh out of the east, and shineth even unto the west, so
shall also the coming of the Son of man be" (24:27). When
I first encountered this verse, it spoke to me concerning the
suddenness of Christ's coming. He is coming, I thought, swift
and powerful. But meteorologists tell us that when lightning

shines from east to west, it has a definite significance. When a storm is approaching, the lightning shines from the west or the northwest. When lightning shines from the east to west, that means the storm is over. Actually, lightning shining from east to west is the rainbow at night. Applied in this instance, the verse seems not only to teach the suddenness of his coming but reveals the glorious fact that when he comes, the storms of life have passed. The storm of death is over. The storm of war is over. The storm of sickness is over. When Jesus comes, the bitter frustrations and limitations that make life difficult shall be a thing of the past. Even so, come, Lord Jesus.

In the closing verse of the sixteenth chapter of Matthew we have a strange utterance. Jesus said: "There be some standing here, which shall not taste of death, till they see the Son of man coming in his kingdom" (16:28). He was speaking to his own disciples when he framed this prophecy. We know that these men died, and Christ has not returned. What then is the meaning of this mysterious verse? The answer is to be found in the first verse of the following chapter. Jesus took Peter, James, and John up the mountain of transfiguration. One can never understand this passage of Scripture unless he realizes that this is a preview of the second coming. This is a rehearsal of the future in miniature. And here, Peter, James, and John were given a glimpse into the future.

Jesus appears before them in transfigured glory, and by his side are Moses and Elijah in conversation with him. The glorious Christ is seen in his second coming attire. To me, Moses and Elijah symbolize the two groups who will be with him in that day. Moses represents the believers who have died in the faith and will experience a resurrection when Christ returns. Elijah, on the other hand, represents the living Christian who will experience translation, not resurrection, because, even as Elijah, they did not die. I have a Christian brother who went to be with Christ during World War II. If Christ were to return in this hour, my brother would be in the group with Moses; I would be in the crowd with Elijah.

In the famous resurrection chapter, 1 Corinthians 15, we have a demonstration of this truth. Paul tells us that when Christ returns, he will smite death with resurrection. He concludes by exclaiming, "O death, where is thy sting? O grave, where is thy victory? But thanks be to God, which giveth us the victory through our Lord Jesus Christ" (vv. 55, 57). Notice the beauty of the double anthems. "O death, where is thy sting?" Only the living Christians, who will not die but will be alive when Christ returns, can sing this part. Our mothers and fathers and loved ones who have died cannot sing this part. But they can surely sing, "O grave, where is thy victory?" They died and were buried, but the grave did not hold them. So, the group with Elijah will sing, "O death, where is thy sting?" and the crowd with Moses will sing, "O grave, where is thy victory?" Then together, we shall sing the chorus: "Thanks be to God, which giveth us the victory through our Lord Jesus Christ." Hallelujah!

He Is Coming Back in Vengeance

We are told in 2 Thessalonians that Jesus will be revealed in flaming fire taking vengeance upon them that know not God (1:8). In Revelation, John informs us that "every eye shall see him, and they also which pierced him: and all kindreds of the earth shall wail because of him" (1:7). This is a truth that we must emphasize. While the coming of Christ will be glory for the child of God, it will be disaster for the unsaved man who refused to face the Christ of mercy and love.

The second coming of Christ will be a tragic time for the man who disregarded moral law and lived as though Christ had not died. We have multitudes in our nation who have no concern for the Ten Commandments and live as if these have no bearing on our lives. Crowds of people disregard the church and treat it with indifference. We are not living in a day when people fight the church; they just ignore it. The Bible has no message for them; the Holy Spirit is not a reality. They are not sure of heaven, but they are sure that hell does not exist. The coming of our Lord will be a revelation of fury for people of this type.

The second coming of Christ will also be tragic for the good moral man who has rested his spiritual interests in moral and ethical achievements. The Word of God encourages men to live right, but at the same time it informs them that mere right living is no substitute for salvation. We are not saved by works of righteousness which we have done, but according to God's mercy redemption becomes our possession. Yet there are multitudes who are placing their hope in their own human righteousness. The coming of our Lord will be a devastating event to those who have not been truly redeemed.

The second coming of Christ will be a time of weeping and despair for the unsaved church member. Jesus told us that in that day many shall come and say, "Didn't we cast out devils in thy name? Have we not prophesied in thy name and in thy name performed wonderful works?" Christ will say unto them, "Depart from me, I never knew you." It is not enough to be a church member. Once a man walked up to a minister friend of mine in a hotel lobby and said: "Are you a minister?" My friend replied in the affirmative. The man then inquired, "In what church do you exercise your ministry?" My friend informed him that he was a Baptist. The man countered, "Oh, you are a Baptist; you are a member of that narrow church that believes that only your gang is going to heaven." My friend replied, "You are wrong, I am more narrow than that. I don't believe some of my gang are going to make it." It is not enough to be a church member.

The second coming of Christ will be a time of distress for the procrastinator. Good intentions will not be acceptable in that hour. It is not enough to affirm one's need of the redeeming love of Christ. The sinner must appropriate it. But how many postpone to a mythical tomorrow that which ought to be done today. The Word of God is constant in urging men to accept now. The Catholics get around the fact that the dying thief was saved without baptism because he had what they call "the baptism of desire." That is, he would have been baptized later if he had lived. But mere desire to be saved is not enough. Men and women must not put off their redemption until the future. One of the greatest sins that we can commit against Christ is to postpone him. The coming of our Lord will be a tragic moment for this group.

In the light of Christ's imminent return, the Christian should be busy with that which is important. Our time should be spent in majoring on majors. This is no time for parochial Christian living. What a glorious privilege is ours—to live between the two mountain peaks of history: Christ's crucifixion and his coronation. That is why Paul could tell the Corinthians, "Knowing therefore the terror of the Lord, we persuade men" (2 Cor. 5:11). Since the wrath of the Lamb (and what a provocative figure) shall be as intense as his love was tender, we must be up and doing the Father's business.

When Jesus ascended into heaven, the lonely disciples continued to gaze into the clouds. The two men in white apparel came to remind them that there was work to do. Before his departure Jesus had told them to be his witnesses in Jerusalem, Judea, and to the uttermost parts of the earth. That was their job; it is also ours. Notice, he said that we were to be his witnesses, not his lawyers. We are not to argue the case. The souls of men are not to be won by a scintillating syllogism. Only as we relate what Christ has done and will do in our present lives can we win the sinner to the Saviour. Our appeal is to be existential; the world demands a demonstration. People who believe the gospel should behave the gospel. Creed and conduct, deed and doctrine, should go hand in hand. And John tells us that he that has this hope within him purifies himself even as Christ is pure.

I boarded a plane sometime ago to return to my waiting family. I happened to sit by a young lady who was in a very joyful mood. Upon inquiring as to her destination, she informed me that she was going to California. Then she added, "I am going to be married. My fiance will be waiting for me at the airport, and we will be man and wife in just a few hours." Then she exclaimed, "Would you like to see his picture?" I could only reply in the affirmative. She opened her purse and began to ramble through a lot of debris in the attempt to find the photograph.

Finally, she located the picture and said to me: "Look at him, isn't he handsome?" I swallowed hard and then told her, "He is," although he was as ugly a man as I had ever seen. All during the trip she talked about Bob; her conversation centered around him. When I arrived at my destination I was so happy to get rid of Bob. Elvis Presley or Rock Hudson could have been on that plane, and she would have never looked at them. She was on her way to marry Bob.

When I got off the plane I thought to myself, she wearied me with her enthusiasm, but that's the way it ought to be. She is in love. Then I thought, the church is going to a wedding. We are on the way. I wonder if we are talking about Jesus on the way. We have a book called the Bible which contains a photograph of our beloved on every page. Are we showing that picture to the people around us? So many of us are flirting with the world. May God help us to be faithful to him in this hour.

2
"When He Shall Appear"

PAUL S. JAMES

BISHOP Arthur J. Moore of The Methodist Church has said, "Recent events do not discredit Christianity; they demand it." This is but another way of saying that many people are asking whether there is a way out of the present situation in the world. They want to know whether God is interested in their plight and, if so, what he is going to do about it. Indeed, Christianity is demanded, for Christianity is the revelation of what God in Christ has done, is doing, and will do.

James Stewart of Edinburgh was recently asked what, in his opinion, will be the main emphasis in preaching during the next decade. Without hesitation he replied, "Eschatology." Two other noted theologians standing in the group quickly agreed with this. Certainly a consideration of what the Bible teaches about the return of our Lord is most timely.

Three Times "Behold!"

"Behold, thy king cometh," the Old Testament declares (Zech. 9:9). Time and again we find prophecies here concerning a messianic kingdom which will be the confirmation of Old Testament covenants that God made with his people. So well was this understood in the time of Christ that even

16

John the Baptist, after introducing our Lord to his public ministry, asked: "Art thou he that should come? or look we for another?" (Luke 7:19). "He came, he came, Emmanuel, to ransom captive Israel that mourns in lonely exile here." The Son of God did appear, but his own people wouldn't receive him. The gospel was first preached to the Jews, then to the Gentiles, in order "to take out of them a people for his name" (Acts 15:14). And to this agree the words of the prophets, as it is written, "After this I will return, and will build again the tabernacle of David, which is fallen down" (v. 16). The prophesied King came in humility and was rejected; he will come again in glory and will reign, for every eye shall see him and every knee will bow to him. Pilate's prophetic inscription over our crucified Lord was in mockery, but he will yet be revealed as King of the Jews in reality.

> Lo, He comes, with clouds descending,
>   Once for favored sinners slain;
> Thousand thousand saints attending
>   Swell the triumph of His train:
>   Alleluia, alleluia!
> God appears on earth to reign.

CHARLES WESLEY

"Behold, I shew you a mystery" (1 Cor. 15:51), Paul writes. Bible mysteries are sacred secrets which are revealed in the fulness of God's time. In the historical development of God's purpose Christ will return. It will be the period at the end of the last sentence of the last paragraph of history. This is, indeed, the one divine event toward which the whole creation moves, and the Bible associates many wonderful things with this event. The renewing of creation is one of them. The transformation of the body is another. Note, for instance, Philippians 3:20-21: "Our conversation (*politeuma*, politics) is in heaven; from whence also we look for the Saviour, the

Lord Jesus Christ: Who shall change our vile body." And 1
Thessalonians 4:16-17: "The Lord himself shall descend from
heaven . . . and the dead in Christ shall rise first: . . . so
shall we ever be with the Lord."

"Behold, I come quickly" is the final promise of the Bible
(Rev. 22:7). "Surely I am coming soon" (22:20, RSV). The
last prayer of the Bible is, "Even so, come, Lord Jesus." Christ
taught his own to expect his return (Mark 13:35-37; Luke
12:35-36), and the early Christians had this as their blessed
hope (1 Tim. 6:14; James 5:8-9). If the coming of the Lord
drew nigh for them, how much closer that coming is for us!

Here, then, are three aspects of our Lord's return: it will
be the coming of the King; it will be the fulfilling of God's
redemptive purpose; and it will be the revelation of him whom
having not seen we love.

He Is Coming

To be sure, Christ's return is frequently presented as a
"coming." "As in the days that were before the flood . . . so
shall also the coming of the Son of man be" (Matt. 24:38-39).
"Watch ye therefore: for ye know not when the master of
the house cometh, at even, or at midnight, or at the cockcrowing, or in the morning . . . I say unto all, Watch"
(Mark 13:35-37). "If I go and prepare a place for you, I will
come again, and receive you unto myself; that where I am,
there ye may be also" (John 14:3). "Ye men of Galilee, why
stand ye gazing up into heaven? this same Jesus . . . shall so
come in like manner as ye have seen him go into heaven"
(Acts 1:11). "There shall come out of Sion the Deliverer,
and shall turn away ungodliness from Jacob: For this is my
covenant unto them, when I shall take away their sins" (Rom.
11:26-27). "Behold, I come as a thief. Blessed is he that
watcheth, and keepeth his garments, lest he walk naked, and
they see his shame" (Rev. 16:15).

This gives us the picture of a Roman sentry supposed to be on guard duty through the night. He becomes weary and slumps down. Presently he is sound asleep. The captain of the guard discovers him in this condition and grabs his tunic from him without waking him. When he rouses his shame is evident. In military court he is condemned as a man who didn't keep his garments; he went to sleep when he should have been watching. So we are exhorted to "watch" in view of our Lord's coming: "Let your loins be girded about, and your lights burning; and ye yourselves like unto men that wait for their Lord" (Luke 12:35-36). We ought to be as spiritually alert as though Christ died yesterday, arose this morning, and is coming back tonight!

The Great Unveiling

In addition to the verses which speak of the coming, there are many others which indicate the nature of his coming and present it as a great appearing. "When Christ, who is our life, shall appear, then shall ye also appear with him in glory" (Col. 3:4). "Keep this commandment without spot, unrebukeable, until the appearing of our Lord Jesus Christ" (1 Tim. 6:14). "Henceforth there is laid up for me a crown of righteousness, which the Lord . . . shall give . . . unto all them also that love his appearing" (2 Tim. 4:8). "Looking [even as Simeon and Anna looked for Christ's first coming] for that blessed hope, and the glorious appearing of the great God and our Saviour Jesus Christ" (Titus 2:13). "Unto them that look for him shall he appear the second time without sin unto salvation" (Heb. 9:28)—which says that all who look for him will not be disappointed. "When the chief Shepherd shall appear, ye shall receive a crown of glory that fadeth not away" (1 Peter 5:4).

The nature of this appearing is spelled out in the title of the last book of the Bible, as well as in separate texts. The final book of the Bible is "the revelation of Jesus Christ." Here we see him as the living Christ in the midst of his churches, the Lamb on the throne, the sovereign Lord who is able to reveal the secret of history, the King of kings. Paul writes of the time "when the Lord Jesus shall be revealed from heaven with his mighty angels" (2 Thess. 1:7), and Peter writes: "Gird up the loins of your mind, be sober, and hope to the end for the grace that is to be brought unto you at the revelation of Jesus Christ" (1 Peter 1:13). The incarnation involves limitation. In Christ, as he lived among men, dwelt "all the fulness of the Godhead bodily" (Col. 2:9). Here was all of God that could be revealed in flesh, and "we beheld his glory, the glory as of the only begotten of the Father, full of grace and truth" (John 1:14). But still it was glory within the limitations of flesh.

The Unseen Glory

Something beyond this was shown to the disciples who were with Christ on the mount of transfiguration. Luke says, "they saw his glory" (9:32). This was a glory greater than the glory they had seen in Christ at any time before, and "as they came down from the mountain, he charged them that they should tell no man what things they had seen, till the Son of man were risen from the dead" (Mark 9:9). The word Jesus used here for "tell" is significant. He didn't use the word which means to tell a thing as a herald announces it—like Paul Revere riding down the valley warning of the coming of the British. Neither did he use the word which means to tell a thing the way a lover tells his love to the one he loves.

Rather, he used the word which means to tell as a gossiper tells some choice bit of information. He was saying in effect: "Don't go down now and tell them how bright the light was and how white the garments were. Don't gossip about this. Indeed, say nothing about it until the Son of man is risen from the dead, for then you will understand what you cannot understand now."

So it was as far as Peter is concerned, for in his second letter he writes:

We have not followed cunningly devised fables, when we made known unto you the power and coming of our Lord Jesus Christ, but were eyewitnesses of his majesty. For he received from God the Father honour and glory, when there came such a voice to him from the excellent glory, This is my beloved Son, in whom I am well pleased. And this voice which came from heaven we heard, when we were with him in the holy mount (2 Peter 1:16-18).

In other words, what he saw of the preincarnate glory of our Lord gave him "the word of prophecy made more sure" as it relates to the glory of Christ which is to be revealed at his second coming. Indeed, "You should give that word your closest attention, for it shines like a lamp amidst all the dirt and darkness of the world, until the day dawns, and the morning star rises in your hearts" (2 Peter 1:19, Phillips).

Awaiting the Bridegroom

In the Olivet discourse (Matthew 24-25) Jesus gave the broad perspective which shows the destruction of Jerusalem in the foreground and the events preceding his return in the distance. He warned against being misled by those who would come in his name, claiming to be Christ. He spoke of the evolution of war: from one nation rising against another nation to the sort of thing we have had in recent international struggles, where one group of nations has been arrayed against another grouping of nations. He told of the spread of wickedness "when many will lose their faith . . . and the love of most men will grow cold" (Matthew 24:10-12, Phillips). He said, "This good news of the kingdom will be proclaimed to men all over the world as a witness to all nations, and then the end will come" (v. 14, Phillips). Should it not give us pause that this has been fulfilled in our time as in no other time—man's intrusion for the first time into "the powers of the heavens" (Matthew 24:29), the "distress of nations, with perplexity" (Luke 21:25) upon the earth, history moving at the speed of jet-propelled planes? The optimism with which the twentieth century was greeted has been largely replaced by dark doubts, and men's hearts are failing them for fear "looking after those things which are coming on the earth" (Luke 21:26).

Here also Christ pictures the separation which will take place at his coming: two in the field, one taken and one left; two grinding at the mill, one taken and the other left; ten virgins, five ready and the others left. It is important to note that the five virgins who were left professed to have something they didn't possess. Their lamps symbolize Christian witness. When the bridegroom's coming was announced they readily trimmed their wicks; but in the showdown it was too bad and too late, for they were essentially unprepared and were shut out. So it is terribly possible to deceive ourselves into the snug belief that to bear a name is enough, to have a lamp is sufficient, to go forth in the company of the people of God is adequate—all the time lacking that inner experience of Christ which will enable us to stand unashamed before him at his coming.

Scoffers Before the Last Day

In the Olivet discourse Christ also says: "As the days of Noe were, so shall also the coming of the Son of man be" (Matt. 24:37). We remember that in those days the majority scoffed while a righteous man prepared for what God told him was coming. In 2 Peter 3:3-4 we are told that scoffers shall come in the last days, "walking after their own lusts, and saying, Where is the promise of his coming?" These wilfully ignorant men base their ridicule of the second coming of Christ on the premise that "all things continue as they were from the beginning" (v. 4), which, of course, isn't true. For one thing, Peter says, the flood came as a cataclysmic change in the course of human events. He then tells of a coming judgment by fire in which the elements will melt with fervent heat. The skeptics used to laugh when the old-time evangelists preached on this text, wondering where all the matches would come from to start the conflagration. The laughter has died down, for today the scientists have become the preachers.

More than once in this passage Peter uses the word meaning to loosen, here translated "dissolved." This word is used in other places in the New Testament concerning the loosening of sandals, of the tongue of a mute, of the colt tied at the crossroads, and of Lazarus who was bound with graveclothes. Is not this an accurate description of the release of atomic power in which the invisible bands that hold electrons, protons, and neutrons inside the atom are broken and these component parts of matter are loosed? It will be the coming of the day of the Lord, and we are to "be diligent that . . . [we] may be found of him in peace, without spot, and blameless" (2 Peter 3:14) as we look for "new heavens and a new earth, wherein dwelleth righteousness" (v. 13).

"Awake, Bright Flame!"

The story of Agamemnon by Aeschylus, the father of Greek tragedy, opens with the soliloquy of a sentry who paces the flat roof of the royal palace at Argos. Nine years have passed since Agamemnon, the head of a federation of Greek states, set out with his armies and a thousand ships to reduce the city of Troy. On the roof of the palace is an unlit beacon, built to be lit when the king returns. Apostrophizing the beacon, the soldier exclaims:

Awake, bright flame!
Herald of joy, burst through the gloom of night.

As he utters the word, a tongue of flame shoots up from the crest of a distant hill. It is the long-expected signal. The soldier shouts in ecstasy:

Rejoice, Rejoice! Hail, thou auspicious flame,
That streaming through the night proclaimest joy!

The long watch is ended, the victory has been won, and the king returns to his own.

Looking and Occupying

Thus do believers wait, mindful of the striking parallel between the first coming and the second coming of Christ. The first coming was long promised, as is true of the second coming. Christ came the first time on schedule: "when the fulness of the time was come" (Gal. 4:4). Though only the Father knows the hour that Christ will come again, it will be "when the fulness of the time" has come. When he came the first time, many went on living as though he had not come; when he comes the second time, many will be living as though he would never come. But there were some looking for his first advent, and there are some looking for his second advent. His first coming ushered in the new day of grace, and his second coming will usher in the new day of righteousness.

His charge, "Occupy till I come" (Luke 19:13), should be to each of us a challenge to keep busy in the exercise of our stewardship. We ought to do our best in evangelism and missions, making every day count as though it might be the last day before the Lord of the harvest returns.

There's a King and Captain high
Who'll be comin' by-and-by,

And He'll find me hoein' cotton when He comes.
You will hear His legions chargin'
In the thunders of the sky,
    And He'll find me hoein' cotton when He comes.

When He comes, when He comes,
All the dead will rise in answer to His drums,
While the fires of his encampment
Star the firmament on high,
    And the heavens are rolled asunder when He comes.

There's a man they thrust aside
Who was tortured till He died,
    And He'll find me hoein' cotton when He comes.
He was hated and rejected,
He was scourged and crucified,
    And He'll find me hoein' cotton when He comes.

When He comes, when He comes
He'll be ringed with saints and angels when He comes.
They'll be shoutin' out hosannas
To the man that men denied,
    And I'll kneel among my cotton when He comes.

BERTRAND SHADWELL

3
The Latter Days

CLYDE T. FRANCISCO

THE most conspicuous difference between the thought of the Hebrews and that of their neighbors is found in the emphasis of the Old Testament on the purpose of God in history. Events are moving toward a goal not yet attained; God is sternly determined to reach his objectives for mankind. Nations are clay in the potter's hand (Jer. 18:1-11). They may resist God's purpose and refuse to do his will, but this will not deter him from moving forward.

All other ancient people shared the common idea that the clue to life was the regular rhythm of the cycle of the year. As winter came on, followed by spring, it could be seen that nature moved in regular circles, not a straight line. All religion became bound up in this concept. The objective of religion was to guarantee the annual coming of the spring rains and consequent fertility of the crops. In more urbanized communities the stress would be put upon the necessity of living in harmony with the settled round of nature. Thus, religion became the defender of the status quo.

It was quite different in Hebrew prophetic thought, although often the priests and common people were tempted to fall victim to the concepts of their heathen neighbors. Because Hebrew was essentially the Canaanite language, it was inevitable that the average person would be tempted to accept the Canaanite concepts along with the language. At this point was the greatest tension between the great prophets and their people. The average Israelites saw no problem in paying homage to the Canaanite nature gods in order to guarantee good crops as well as human fertility. The Lord was still the supreme God of Israel and of history. The prophets, however, were adamant in their opposition to this interest in the nature gods. They clearly saw that in addition to the immorality that was always associated with this type of worship, there was the temptation to lose sight of the true nature of life itself. Religion would be used as a means of adjustment to vested institutions in society. Its resources would be dedicated to keeping anyone from disturbing the regular rhythm of society's established patterns. God would be guest of honor at their feasts but not the righteous judge of their conduct.

Thus there could be no compromise with nature religion in Israel. Only the Lord could be served. It was he who sat in judgment upon them, making decisions upon the basis of their response to his purpose in history.

It is significant that the purpose of God for man is made clear in the opening chapter of the Bible: "Be fruitful, and multiply, and replenish the earth, and subdue it: and have dominion over the fish of the sea, and over the fowl of the air, and over every living thing that moveth upon the earth" (Gen. 1:28). Man is to bring all the earth under his dominion in the name of his God. As a great king appoints a governor of a province and instructs him to rule in his name, so God commissioned man to rule the earth. He is to have dominion but not in his own right. It is to be achieved under God and for his glory.

Man may have a different idea about his own objectives. He may decide to build great projects to bring glory to him-

self, concerned only about his own name, as in the occasion of
the building of the tower of Babel. Such folly is always re-
warded by the judgment of God. Man will never be allowed
to pursue his own objective, leaving God out of his plans.
God will continue to work until the whole universe has been
brought into subjection to him. And he wills for all men to
accomplish this purpose. It may seem to man that God is not
at work in history and that the process is intolerably slow
(Hab. 2:3). Yet, slowly and consistently God is directing the
affairs of men toward his avowed goal. Of necessity the process is unhurried, for God is committed to permitting men to
make their own free choices. Such a relationship between
leader and people is always comparatively slow, but who can
deny the superiority of the results ultimately to be attained?

Numerous are the passages in the Old Testament describing
the glories of the future age that God will one day bring to
pass. Invariably the scene will take place on this earth with
Jerusalem as the hub of all activity (Mic. 4:1 ff.). The land
of Palestine, once flowing with milk and honey but now
devastated by wars, drought, and land monopoly, will become
like the Garden of Eden (Ezek. 36:30, 35; Amos 9:13). There
will be new heavens and a new earth, but something of the
old will still remain also (Isa. 65:17-25).

Along with the remarkable fertility of the land will occur
an enormous population explosion in keeping with the promise of Genesis 22:17. Such passages as Hosea 1:10 and Isaiah
54:1-3 emphasizes this. Part of this new population will be
those who have been raised from the dead (Isa. 26:13-19).

The people who survive to live in this new age are both
Jew and Gentile who honor the Lord (Isa. 66:19 ff.).
Zephaniah puts it plainly: "I will also leave in the midst of
thee an afflicted and poor people, and they shall trust in the
name of the Lord" (Zeph. 3:12). As for the Gentiles, "The
Lord will be terrible unto them: for he will famish all the

gods of the earth; and men shall worship him, every one from his [own] place, even all the isles of the heathen" (Zeph. 2:11).

Both Jeremiah (31:31 ff.) and Ezekiel (36:25 ff.) describe the characteristics of the people who live in the ideal age to come. The law of God will be written upon their hearts, rather than on tables of stone. In other words, the impulse to serve God will come from within (Jer. 31:33). Each man will have a personal experience with God and will live in a harmonious community of pardoned sinners. The ideal society will continue unspoiled forever. Ezekiel adds that not only will the law of God be put in the heart but also a new heart will be given to man, so that the law will remain uncorrupted (Ezek. 36:26). The reason why this new relationship with God will be lasting is because the Lord will put his own Spirit within them and will himself enable them to live as he purposes (Ezek. 36:27).

Such ideal people, although made up of many nations, will live together in the world in harmony. The most remarkable result will be that the two Jewish nations, Judah and Israel, will cease their hostilities and become one (Jer. 3:18; Ezek. 37:15-28; Zech. 10:6-12). Many passages stress the ready and willing submission of the Gentiles to the rule of the Jews (Isa. 14:1-3; 49:22-23; 60:10; Zech. 8:20 ff.). But a significant number also hint at the future equality of the nations in the age to come (Amos 9:7; Isa. 19:23-25; 56:1-6; 66:18-21; Zech. 9:6-7; Psalm 87).

The last enemy that shall be destroyed is death. In a beautiful passage in Isaiah 25:8 it is said: "He will swallow up death in victory; and the Lord God will wipe away tears from off all faces; and the rebuke of his people shall he take away from off all the earth: for the Lord hath spoken it."

Such, then, is the purpose of God in history. By patience and judgment he is determined to establish his dominion over all the earth. He will continue to work until he has produced a people who will reflect his righteous character. Once established, this rule will be permanent. Universal peace will at long last be achieved and will last forever. All the enemies of man will be conquered, even the power of death. The mouth of the Lord has spoken it. Therefore it must come to pass. As in the original creation God had only to speak and it was so, even so in history his word will not return unto him void (Isa. 55:11).

How will this great purpose of God be accomplished? It will be through his chosen agents, whom he elects to carry out his will. The first eleven chapters of Genesis show man hopelessly ensnared in sin. Even righteous Noah backslides and can only hope in the grace of God. What can be done to effect the ultimate purpose of God? Abraham is chosen to be the instrument through whom God will bless the whole world (Gen. 12:1-3). When he and his family are circumcised, a new beginning is made in redemption (chap. 17), for now we have a chosen family.

It was not until the Exodus from Egypt that the Hebrew nation was born. Then a covenant was made for the first time between God and a people (Ex. 19:3-6). God elected a nation through whom to work his will for mankind. It is of major significance, however, that the covenant with Abraham was unconditional, while the one with Israel was conditional. As Abraham left his kindred to follow wherever God might lead, God guaranteed that he would be his chosen instrument. Israel, however, would be his peculiar treasure only if they obeyed his voice. The continuation of the covenant depended upon their keeping their part of it. If they would be faithful to God, then he would use them.

The history that follows is an unfolding tragedy. God's chosen nation, in spite of the pleas of the great prophets, refused to fulfil their mission. They turned a deaf ear and a stubborn shoulder toward their Lord. They tried to enjoy his blessing without assuming their responsibilities. Accordingly, the nation was crushed and exiled. Did this mean that the covenant between God and Israel had been made void by their failure? Legally, yes. Israel deserved to be cut off. But the God who loved them could not bear to do this. Yet the old impasse could not be condoned. What was there to do?

Out of the heartbreak of rejection and inner suffering, Jeremiah came to see the way God had chosen (31:31 ff.). Although Israel deserved to be cast off as the chosen of God (v. 32), the Lord would not reject them. With the old covenant hopelessly broken, thus becoming null and void, God would make a new one. This one, too, would be made with Israel, but it would be guaranteed by God. Like the one with Abraham, it would stand forever.

Did this mean that the new covenant would be made with every Jew? Isaiah 65:8-16 clearly shows that not all the Jews will accept the Suffering Servant of chapter 53. It is the believing remnant of Israel that God elects, his "servants" who are the seed of the great Servant. The old name of God's people becomes a curse, and a new name is given them (65:15). In other words, God makes the new covenant with Israel when the Suffering Servant calls his faithful followers. Those who follow him are the true Israel. They are Israelites, descendants of Abraham, Isaac, and Jacob, but also faithful men.

When Jesus gathered his loyal band about him at the Last Supper, he taught that now the new covenant predicted by Jeremiah was to be inaugurated in the shedding of his blood (Matt. 26:28). When the fellowship of the first disciples with their Saviour was sealed by his death and resurrection, the new covenant had been made with Israel. In Revelation 12 we find that not only does the woman Israel give birth to the Messiah, but also the persecuted followers of Jesus Christ are the "remnant of her seed."

The hope of redemption for all Israel, therefore, is not to be found in nonbelieving Israelites, no matter how organized, but in the remnant of Israel who combine with the Gentile believers in the church. They are the men with whom the new covenant is made, not merely Israel after the flesh. It will be through this chosen people that the rest of Israel will be won to Christ, not by the physical nation with whom there is no longer a covenant. God will not rest until all Israel is saved, but he will do it through his chosen church, not a self-appointed unbelieving state.

The formation of the state of Israel may be a sign of the fulfilment of God's purpose. However, this offers little hope until the true Israel, the church, can find a hearing there. Salvation for the Jews, as well as the Gentiles, comes after hearing the gospel. And how shall they hear without a preacher? When his disciples asked Jesus whether he would at that time return the kingdom to Israel, he replied with a charge to preach the gospel to all the world (Acts 1:6-8). How else could the restoration ever take place?

Any consideration of the picture of the ideal age in the Old Testament must also include a study of its teaching concerning a personal Messiah. It is debatable that the Hebrew term "Messiah" (English: Anointed One; Greek: *Christos)* is used in the Old Testament as a title of the Ideal One to come. The only possibility is Daniel 9:25-26 where some argue that the term even here is still to be translated "an anointed one," rather than "Messiah," and refers to a priest during the Maccabean revolt. This writer finds it difficult to understand the passage except as depicting the personal Messiah of the ideal age but is forced to admit that the case remains debatable. Whether the term "Messiah" as a proper name originates after the time of the book of Daniel or in the above passage must remain undetermined. However, the Old Testament anticipation of an Ideal One to come is quite apparent.

The concept of a personal deliverer to usher in the ideal age seems to be rooted in the reign of David. The great disappointment that came because of the failure of his descendants was offset by the expectation that one day a second David would appear and establish a perpetual reign of righteousness.

This form of the hope for the future was particularly strong in the eighth century. Isaiah 7:14 and 9:6-7 are of major significance. In 7:14 the coming of Immanuel ("God with us") is forecast to the house of David. Who is this Immanuel? The best clue is in 9:7 where the mysterious child is pictured as a son of David ruling on his throne. In face of the evident failure of the recent king, God is about to send an Ideal One who will truly effect the righteous purpose of the Lord.

How is this ideal king described? First, he is born of an *almah*. The Hebrew term clearly means "a mature young woman," whether a virgin or not. Is she a virgin here, or the wife of Ahaz, or even Isaiah's wife? One cannot tell with finality from the Hebrew passage itself. The balance of meaning is tipped by the Greek Septuagint, whose translators render the word *parthenos,* "virgin." In other words, they are convinced that she is a virgin. What convinced them? No one knows today, but it was the Septuagint that was quoted by Matthew (1:23). The term virgin, then, is not a translation of the Hebrew word *almah* but an interpretation of the word from the context.

Perhaps the best explanation of the interpretation is the evident overtone of deity applied to the One to come. His name is "God with us." He will also be called "mighty God." In a parallel passage Micah says his "goings forth have been from old, from everlasting" (5:2); that is, he has been active in delivering Israel before he is born in Bethlehem. Some would translate "goings forth" as "origin" or "beginnings," but this would be more characteristic of Greek than Hebrew thought. In fact, the term is used only one other time in the

Old Testament (2 Kings 10:27). There it means a privy (a place to which one goes forth), and the emphasis is far from being upon "origin."

If in some sense, then, the second David would be divine, how else would he be born except of a virgin? The ancient Near Eastern world could think in no other terms. That this was perceived by the Greek translators of the Hebrew passage seems quite probable. At any length, the two versions together give clear witness to the fact that the mother will be a mature young woman who is also a virgin.

In the second place, his coming is anticipated as occurring in the near future. Before Immanuel will reach moral maturity, Rezin and Pekah will lose their thrones. In ten years both these kings were gone. The Deliverer of Isaiah 9:6 comes at the close of the Assyrian conflict. Some would contend that this proves that the two passages are not messianic or if they are that Isaiah was not a true prophet.

The truth of the matter is that the prophets always saw the ideal age just around the corner, in very much the way that the New Testament saints regarded the return of Christ as always imminent. It is like standing upon a mountain and looking across at the ranges ahead. They seem close enough to reach in a short walk, but are really separated by miles. One does not realize the distance until he starts walking it.

To the prophets the events of the coming kingdom were so certain and sure that they were always just upon them. Isaiah was surely speaking of the Messiah, but it would take longer for him to arrive than Isaiah fully realized. How he described him is accurate in every degree, but to finite man God's time is always beyond one's grasp. It will be noted that history does not contradict Isaiah, however. These two kings are gone before the Messiah matures, although the time between the events is centuries longer than the prophet realized. Pekah and Rezin had no longer to rule than Isaiah foresaw.

Daniel deals with the same problem. Jeremiah had predicted that Jerusalem would lie desolate before Babylonia for seventy years (Dan. 9:2). Now these years had almost passed. Would God fulfil his word? Jerusalem is to be rebuilt immediately (v. 24), but it will take not just seventy years to complete the restoration but seventy times seven—much longer than anticipated. The solution of the sin problem is more complicated than any man can ever realize.

In the third place, the second David will inaugurate a reign of righteousness that will never end. He will be the one who ushers in the eternal age of peace, the Messianic Age (Isa. 9:7). Until he comes there is no escape from the discouraging cycle of sin, judgment, repentance, and sinning again.

As the years went by, those who kept hoping that the next king would be the Great Deliverer became more and more disappointed in the actual sons of David. Even if a king was righteous, his sons would undo his contributions after he was gone. Could mere kingly power accomplish the solution to the problem of sin?

The answer is to be found in Isaiah 52:13 to 53:12. The coming Deliverer must be more than a Davidic king endowed with the power of deity. He must also be Saviour. There are those who would argue against this interpretation of the passage. They would say that the Suffering Servant is not the Davidic Messiah. Rather, he is the personification of Israel who is the hope of the world—its savior.

Such interpretations ignore two plain facts. In the first place, the work of the Servant is identified with the covenant with David (Isa. 55:1-3). In fact, David (the second David) is to do the work of the Servant (vv. 4-5). The Suffering Servant is the Davidic Deliverer, who now not only rules but redeems.

In the second place, the Servant cannot be Israel, for the prophet, himself an Israelite, benefits from the sacrifice of the

Servant. It is the prophet who speaks in chapter 53, not the Gentiles. This is evident when he calls the Jews "my people" (53:8).

The book of Zechariah also combines the characteristics of King and Saviour in one person. In Zechariah 9:9 the coming King is just (righteous). The Suffering Servant is called "my righteous servant" (Isa. 53:11), the term being repeated twice in the Hebrew. Also he is described as "having salvation," the literal Hebrew being "having been saved"—another quality of the Servant who was apparently defeated but ultimately triumphed. Also he is said to be "lowly" or "afflicted," the same term used in Isaiah 53:7. Plainly the two offices are combined in one person.

In Zechariah 11:1-14 and 13:7-9 we have a description of the rejected and smitten shepherd. The figure of a shepherd in this context applies to a ruler or king. The mortal wounding of the good shepherd is mentioned in 12:10. Who could this be except the King who, although innocent, dies and ultimately redeems his people through the shedding of his blood (Zech. 13:1)?

It is objected that the Jews in the days of Jesus did not combine the two concepts of King and Suffering Servant into one expected person. They viewed the functions to be those of two different "coming Ones." On the whole this was true, but could it not be that they did not properly interpret the Old Testament while Jesus saw what was really there? Besides, some Jews with unusual insight did combine the two concepts into the expectation of one Redeeming King. Such was the view of Simeon (Luke 2:25-35) and Anna (Luke 2:38).

It is evident, therefore, that the Old Testament pictures the second David as in some sense divine. Not only will he rule on David's throne, but he will also be the Saviour from sin. His rejection by his own people will precede his act of salvation and ultimate exaltation. The event of his coming will inaugurate the ideal age of the future. He will begin a reign that will endure forever over all the earth (Zech. 9:9-10).

How is this to be understood in light of the historical events of the New Testament? Jesus was born, he died, he was resurrected, and he returned to the Father. He now reigns over the church, but this will be fully achieved over all men only when he returns in like manner as his departure.

Is there any recognition in the Old Testament of a first and second coming of the Messiah? It can be answered immediately that no such distinctions are ever made. The coming of the Ideal One inaugurates a reign that will eventually extend to all the earth. Nothing is said of his ascension to God and an ultimate return to bring an end to our age of trouble. This is not yet clearly seen. Yet the broad outlines of these events are to be noticed in at least one passage of the Old Testament.

In Micah 5:2-7 the Son of David is born to rule over his people. This he proceeds to do (v. 4). Afterwards, the people over whom he is ruling are attacked and the land is invaded (vv. 5-9), but he defeats their enemies and the benevolent influence of his reign is accomplished upon the earth. Thus two serious crises are seen in the reign of the Ideal King: the event of his coming to reign over his own people, and an ultimate unsuccessful attempt of his enemies to overthrow his kingdom.

These correspond clearly with the two advents of the New Testament: (1) Christ comes to reign over his church; (2) in the last days a final attempt is made to exterminate the saints, ushering in a terrible time of trouble. Jesus' second advent secures permanent worldwide peace and his personal rule. If the millennial age is seen to follow the second advent immediately, to be ended by a last rebellion, this attack proves to be quite abortive and futile (Rev. 20:9), and the saints need never trouble themselves about it. Their primary concern is to endure through the days of trouble preceding the second advent. Once the final age is ushered in, their worries are over.

Thus far we have concerned ourselves with what God purposes in history. What is man's responsibility in light of this, as the Old Testament writers see it?

1. Man must recognize that he is created by God and is God's possession (Psalm 24:1). Gratefully acknowledging his dependence upon God, he is to serve him gladly (Psalm 101:2).

2. Knowing what God purposes in the world, and expecting his intervention momentarily, he will seek in his place of responsibility to work for the same ends. The ideal society God intends to establish in the ultimate age should be approximated by those who serve him in the troubled present (Amos 5:24). The fact that others do not so live is no excuse for the people of God. Because they are known of God, more is expected of them (Amos 3:2). Israel is not to lie on "beds of ease," waiting for God to set things right. They must share God's concern for the afflicted (Amos 6:1-6).

3. Having done what one can do, he must trust God to do the rest. Eventual victory is in God's hands, not man's (Isa. 30:15). If man tries to accomplish his purposes without God's help, he is doomed to eventual failure (Isa. v. 16). He must do what he can, but the victory will belong to God.

Everywhere today people are asking in light of the present world distress, "What can I do? With the population of the world increasing faster than we are winning people to Christ, what can my little contribution mean to the cause of God? With materialism and immorality rampant, how can my weak efforts stem the tide?"

The Old Testament saint would reply that there is very little man can do. Moses could not dry up the Red Sea, but he could urge the priests to take the first step of faith. Joshua could not push down the walls of Jericho, but he could march about the city with a mighty blast of horns. Gideon could not by force of arms rout the Midianites. Yet he could carry his light and shout for God. There was not much they could do, but what they could do, they accomplished with responsible faithfulness. God did the rest.

Man is expected to do no more than he is capable of achieving. The rest is in the hands of God. Just as God had the first word in history, so also he will have the last.

4
Comments Concerning Christ's Coming

ROBERT GREENE LEE

"THIS same Jesus . . . shall so come in like manner as ye have seen him go" (Acts 1:11). As many comments as there are flowers in all the fields and fishes in all the seas of the earth are not adequate to say all that could be said about the greatest fact in prophetic statement, the assurance of the finished program of God—"that blessed hope," even "the glorious appearing of the great God and our Saviour Jesus Christ" (Titus 2:13)—the momentous, mysterious, joyous, instantaneous, visible, victorious, glorious coming again of our blessed Saviour in a personal return that will usher in the millennium.

Concerning Christ

The One who comes is he who, during the days of his flesh on earth, was Son of man without sin and Son of God with power. Christ—"whom he [God] hath appointed heir of all things, by whom also he made the worlds" (Heb. 1:2). Christ —"the brightness of his [God's] glory, and the express image of his person" (Heb. 1:3). Christ—"the image of the invisible God" (Col. 1:15), "in him . . . all fulness dwells" (Col.

1:19). Christ—who "humbled himself, and became obedient unto death, even the death of the cross" (Phil. 2:8). Christ— whom "God also hath highly exalted . . . and given . . . a name which is above every name" (Phil. 2:9). Christ—the incarnation of God's heart.

About this coming-again One, somebody wrote:

Jesus was the verity of God's truth;
Jesus was the beauty of God's holiness;
Jesus was the purity of God's nature;
Jesus was the reality of God's love;
Jesus was the surety of God's promise;
Jesus was the majesty of God's power;
Jesus was the authority of God's throne;
Jesus was the pity of God's heart;
Jesus was the repository of God's fulness;
Jesus was the legacy of God's will;
Jesus was the ocean of all God's full and flowing rivers of grace.

Absolutely sinless was the Christ on whose brow flashed the diadem of world creation, whose hand swayed the scepter of universal authority, whose majesty filled heaven with glory, whose wrath filled hell with terror, whose goodness filled this earth with blessing. His life was a flawless mirror of stainless purity, reflecting the wisdom of God. His incomparable character still shines as earth's purest diamond.

This is the holy and almighty One who is coming again—the One who had glory with his Father before the world was, who was loved by the Father before this world (John 17), who in the eternities was coexistent, coequal, coeternal with God. The One who will come is he who, during the days of his flesh on earth, never struck a jarring note, never was betrayed into an error of judgment, never had a moral fiber loosened by temptation, never let circumstances leave fingerprints upon his character—the Lord of Gethsemane's blood sweat, of Calvary's iron spikes, of the empty tomb where he smashed at one blow death's empire of skulls and skeletons, of the cloud that received him out of sight above Mt. Olive's brow.

Concerning Certainty

The Scriptures, from Genesis to Revelation, tell us he is coming—audibly, visibly, personally, imminently. The Scriptures do not say when he is coming. But if the Bible speaks with more emphasis about any one thing than any other, it is the certainty of Christ's coming again to this earth. His coming is one of the cornerstones upon which the temple of God's plan for the world is erected.

In the Old Testament there are some three hundred and eighty prophecies concerning the coming of Christ for the first time. These stood "as beacon lights on the hills of God's landscape." And about three hundred and seventy verses in the New Testament refer to his coming the second time. The Scriptures everywhere assign towering pre-eminence to Christ's second coming. Christ, the one in whose person centered the ultimate purpose of God, made for himself claims unmistakably divine, true, and final. Christ says he is *coming*, coming in *glory*, coming in *his* glory, coming in *great* glory. Of all the seven to eight thousand verses in the New Testament, one out of every twenty-five points forward with eager gestures to the appearing again of the Lord Jesus. Frequently it is set forth as the great hope of the church, as the promise of promises, as the consummation of all promises, as the coronation of all evangelical and evangelistic hopes, as the sum of all prophecy and prayer.

There is not a Christian virtue for the enforcement of which appeal is not made. How glad and grateful we should be for Jesus' statement, "I come quickly." What immeasurable riches of truth that statement holds. It is a two-thousand-year-old golden deposit to which men have come to secure both spiritual food and garments of righteousness.

Just as surely as Christ was God incarnate, just as surely as Christ's death was redemptive as he "died for our sins according to the scriptures" (1 Cor. 15:3), just as surely as Christ's bodily resurrection was evidence of Christ's authority, the test of Christ's deity, the completion of his work of salvation—just so surely is Christ's coming back to earth again to take over the affairs of the world and complete that which he commenced on Calvary's cross—a coming back which looks to a conquest of the whole earth.

Jesus is coming back to raise the righteous dead and enable the living Christians to be "caught up together with them in the clouds, to meet the Lord in the air" (1 Thess. 4:17). Jesus is coming back to reign in righteousness. Then the present apostasy of the church, the increasing sinfulness of mankind, the problems of our sinful world—war, class, and race; national hatreds and prejudices; industrial injustice, drunkenness, cruelty, ignorance, lust, and greed shall be eradicated—and not by human effort.

There are those who preach and teach that the redemption of mankind rests with science, philosophy, education. So far as religion shall effect such redemption, it will be by preaching against war, capitalism, and nationalism, thereby creating a new social order and changing the world over to become the kingdom of God. All of this is against the entire plan for world redemption—as set forth in the Bible.

When, as Isaiah anticipates, shall men "beat their swords into plowshares, their spears into pruninghooks: nation shall not lift up sword against nation, neither shall they learn war any more"? It is when Jesus in person "shall judge among the nations, and shall rebuke many people" (Isa. 2:4).

When are the kingdoms of this world to become the kingdoms of our Lord and of his Christ (Rev. 11:15)? When, as

Isaiah teaches, "the Lord of hosts shall reign in mount Zion" (24:23); when, as Micah said, "the law shall go forth of Zion, and the word of the Lord from Jerusalem" (4:2); when, as David wrote in his messianic Psalm, "In his days shall the righteous flourish; and abundance of peace so long as the moon endureth. He shall have dominion also from sea to sea and from the river unto the ends of the earth" (Psalm 72:7-8).

Nature and grace alike proclaim a glorified Messiah coming again from heaven, in his almightiness, as indispensable to complete their appointed courses. Nature called for him thus to rectify her unwilling disorder, to repair her shattered structures, to restore her oppressed energies, to vindicate the voice of conscience long despised, to verify her sublime testimony to the Creator as long questioned and overlooked. His coming again is as certain as that God's honor is at stake in every promise he makes. His glorious coming again, with all its attendant circumstances and its effect upon the church, is a sublime motive for evangelistic and missionary activity—not the dreams of ignorant fanatics, not the creation of speculation in theology. It is a divinely revealed truth.

This divinely revealed truth of Christ's regal return should make us grateful for the Confession of Faith put forth by forty leaders and deacons of the General Baptists in England in 1660 and later approved as the standard confession of this group. It was presented to King Charles II in London, and in it was declared:

That the same Lord Jesus who shewed himself alive after his passion, by many infallible proofs, *Acts* 1.3. which was taken up from the Disciples, and carried up into Heaven, *Luke* 24.51. *Shall so come in like manner as he was seen go into Heaven, Acts* 1.9, 10,11. *And when Christ who is our life shall appear, we shall also appear with him in glory, Col.* 3.4. For then shall he be King of Kings, and Lord of Lords, *Rev.* 19.16. for the Kingdom is his, and he is the Governour among the Nations, *Psal.* 22.28. and King over all the earth, *Zech. 14.9. and we shall reign (with him) on the Earth, Rev. 5.10.* the Kingdomes of this World, (which men so mightily strive after here to enjoy) shall become the Kingdomes of our Lord, and his Christ, *Rev. 11.15.*[1]

Concerning their faith, they further said: "We are not only resolved to suffer persecution for the loss of our goods, but also life itself, rather than decline from the same." Grateful are we that these men who were Bible students should so declare themselves as to the truth that, though Christ may refine us in the fires of persecution that will characterize and curse the close of the age, he will bring us at last into his own kingdom, make us subjects of his everlasting love, and celebrate with us one thousand jubilant years on earth as preparatory for the ravaging joys of an eternal heaven.

More marvelous than Pentecostal scenes, more startling than the fall of Jerusalem, more blessed than the indwelling of the Spirit, more blessed than the departure to be with the Lord will be the literal, visible, bodily return of Christ. No event may seem less probable to unaided human reason. No event is more certain in the light of inspired Scripture. "This same Jesus . . . shall so come in like manner as ye have seen him go" (Acts 1:11). "Behold, he cometh with clouds; and every eye shall see him" (Rev. 1:7).

As he appeared to Isaiah in his vision, to the disciples on the holy mount, to Saul on his way to Damascus, to John on Patmos, so surely will the Son of man appear when, as he promised, he is seen "sitting on the right hand of power, and coming in the clouds of heaven" (Matt. 26:64).

[1]William L. Lumpkin, *Baptist Confessions of Faith* (Philadelphia: The Judson Press, 1959), pp. 231-32; note that the phrase "with him" is not in the New Testament but is an insertion by the authors of the confession. Baptist historians trace Baptists of the United States to the Particular rather than the General Baptists of England; Particular Baptist confessions teach the second coming but not a future reign of Christ on earth.

Concerning Conjectures

What some designate as and declare to be Christ's second coming, I term mere conjectures.

1. Christ's second coming is not the spiritual presence of Christ—not a spiritual coming that takes place at regeneration. One of the most comforting and inspiring of truths is the teaching that Christ does come to each believer by his Holy Spirit, dwells within, and empowers for service, suffering, and growth in grace. But this is to be held in harmony with the other blessed truth that Christ will some day literally appear again in bodily form—and "we shall be like him; for we shall see him as he is" (1 John 3:2).

2. The special manifestation of the Holy Spirit at Pentecost did not fulfil the promise of Christ's return. Peter and Paul and other inspired apostles, long after Pentecost, emphasized the coming of Christ as the highest incentive for life and service.

3. The providential events of history, such as the destruction of Jerusalem, are not to be interpreted as the second coming of Christ. Long after this tragedy of history (the capture of the Holy City by Titus) John wrote in Gospel and Apocalypse of the coming of the King.

4. The cataclysmic upheavals of the world are not to be labeled as Christ's second coming. History is his story, and his footprints are seen everywhere in the sands of time. To take Christ out of history is like taking heat out of fire. But the Bible has no such meaning for the coming again of Jesus.

5. Great disturbances in nature are not to be called his second coming. God's power may be revealed, the hand of God may be seen, and the voice of God heard in such disturbances. "Earthquakes may be the tread of his feet, the lightning flashes the light of his eyes, the thunder the sound of his voice, the clouds the dust of his chariot wheels" but this

is not what the Bible means by the coming of Christ to manifest himself to the world.

6. Nor is Christ's second coming his appearing to us in the hour of death. Christ's second coming is not to be confused with death. We know that for the Christian to die is gain. Blessed is the expression "to be absent from the body" and "to be at home with the Lord." But death is inseparable with pain and loss, sorrow and tears. Even those who are now with their Lord in heavenly joy are waiting for their bodies of glory and for the rewards and reunions which will be theirs at the appearing of Christ. I have seen many die, and I have heard quite a number speak in their death hours of seeing Jesus. But that is not what we mean by the second coming of Christ into the world.

7. Christ's second coming is not his conquest in the world with the gospel. His conquests have been glorious, his victories marvelous, the winning power of the gospel manifested everywhere. Christ has made conquests. He is still making conquests. But that is not what the Bible means by Christ's coming again to this world.

Concerning Characteristics

What will occur when Christ does come in his own glory, the glory of the Father, and of the holy angels? What will happen when he who was "despised and rejected of men" returns in power and great glory, attended by thousands of the heavenly hosts?

The first phase of Christ's second coming will be the descent of the Lord from heaven. "The Lord himself shall descend from heaven with a shout, with the voice of the archangel, and with the trump of God" (1 Thess. 4:16).

Then there will be the resurrection and translation of the righteous dead. "The dead in Christ shall rise first" (1 Thess. 4:16)—the dead who were redeemed by him and who died looking for his coming. Literally, it might be translated, the dead in Christ shall stand up first.

Millions whose bodies are sleeping in the earth will hear his voice. As Lazarus, dead in the tomb, heard Christ's voice and immediately sprang to life, so all the saved who have died will stand up—in the first resurrection. The bodies of believers will be raised in glory. The dead will be raised incorruptible and immortal (1 Cor. 15:52-54). "Sown in corruption; it is raised in incorruption: . . . sown in dishonor; it is raised in glory" (vv. 42-43). This is, peculiarly, the resurrection of "the dead in Christ" and has no reference to the resurrection of "the rest of the dead," which takes place later—"the rest of the dead lived not again until the thousand years were finished" (Rev. 20:5). "Then we which are alive and remain shall be caught up together with them in the clouds, to meet the Lord in the air: and so shall we ever be with the Lord" (1 Thess. 4:17).

Both the saved dead and the living believer will be translated together and will meet the descending Lord in the air. Some Christians will never die. One generation of believers will be living when Christ returns. They will be given bodies fashioned like unto Christ's own glorious body and taken up without the experience of death (Phil. 3:21). In this marvelous change they will be clothed upon with the glory of immortality—"In a moment, in the twinkling of an eye, at the last trump: for the trumpet shall sound, and the dead shall be raised incorruptible" (1 Cor. 15:52).

Yes, together the saved dead and living Christians will rise to meet Christ in the air, be greeted by him, and dwell with him, being ever "with the Lord" (1 Thess. 4:17). This is the coming of the bridegroom for the bride. This is followed by the marriage of the Lamb (Rev. 19:7) and the judgment of works (1 Cor. 3:13-15). We shall stand before Christ's judgment seat in our glorified bodies to receive rewards according to the deeds done in this life. The complete recompense of the faithful is "at the resurrection of the just" (Matt. 25 and Luke 19).

Then will come the great tribulation. It will be such as was not since the beginning of the world to this time. (Matt. 24:15; Dan. 12:1). The taking of Christians out of the world will usher in the great tribulation. The two things that will contribute to this are the absence of the Holy Spirit from this earth and the presence of the devil (Rev. 12:12) on earth.

The devil was first cast out of the mountain of God (Ezek. 28:16) into the air (Eph. 2:2). When Jesus comes in the air, the devil is cast down to the earth. Later when Jesus comes to earth to sit upon the throne of his glory (Matt. 25:31), even the throne of David (Luke 1:32), and reign one thousand years, the devil is cast out of the earth into the bottomless pit (Rev. 20:2-3). Thus, in three stages, he reaches his end.

Concerning Conceptions

Here we are concerned with men's conceptions of Christ's coming and the millennium—the time when universal peace shall reign as Christ rules and shall prevail. Because of Revelation 20:4, we call it the "millennium," which is the Latin term for "one thousand years." During the millennium the devil is to be bound—deprived of his power. Around the word "millennium" cluster three important systems of belief.

Postmillennialism is the belief that through the preaching of the gospel, missionary work, and education the world will be won to Christ and a wonderful period of peace and prosperity will be experienced; after which the Lord Jesus will come personally for the final judgment, when both good and bad will be raised and the end of the world will be here. The postmillennium view is the evolutionary view—the view of continuous progress and development in goodness. It is the natural view for the natural man to take. It is the way man would have done it had it been left for man to bring it about. But look at the spiritual condition of the world today. We have had preaching and education for two thousand years, and nine-tenths of the world is non-Christian yet. There isn't a single village in all the world that has yet been converted. How many more thousands of years, at this rate, is it going to take us to convert all the world or even a goodly part of it? Luther said: "Some say that before the last day the world shall become Christian, but it is a falsehood forged by Satan that he might darken sound doctrine."

Premillennialism is the belief that the Lord Jesus Christ will come personally before the millennium, usher it in, and reign over the earth during this time.

Dean Alford, one of the greatest Greek scholars the world has ever known, says: "The majority both in number and learning adopt the pre-millennial advent, following, as it seems to me the plain and undeniable sense of the sacred text of the Bible itself."

Amillennialism is the belief that there will be no literal earthly kingdom of Christ, but that he will come personally to hold the last judgment and to inaugurate the eternal state. Amillennialists hold that the prophecies in the Scriptures concerning a future kingdom for Israel are fulfilled spiritually in the church. Amillennialists believe that there will be no thousand-year period of blessing and peace upon the earth following the return of Christ. They see no golden age, no utopia in the future, but sudden destruction of the world at Christ's second coming.

Amillennialists believe that at the second coming of Christ there will be a cataclysmic destruction of the earth and that the saved and lost will, at that time, enter their eternal state. This view, so it seems to the writer, is arbitrarily propagated in the face of Bible facts contradicting it. Amillennialists believe that the prophetic book of Revelation was written, for the most part, for the comfort of the first-century Christians and was fulfilled in the first and second centuries.

Concerning Censure

There are those who label men—men of integrity and devotion to the cause of Christ, who have won souls through the years, who have rendered faithful service for God—queer, heretical, and unscholarly because they declare the premillennial view of Christ's second coming.

Massillon is quoted as having said: "In the days of primitive Christianity, it would have been deemed a kind of apostasy not to sigh for the return of the Lord." A. J. Gordon remarks: "Strange it is that we have reached an age where it is counted an eccentricity to love Christ's appearance and a theological error to cry with the best-loved apostle, 'Even so, come, Lord Jesus.'"

Yet, mighty men, devoted servants all, before whose eyes the Scriptures have unfolded with the greatest beauty, not only join in that cry, but unite their voices in proclaiming Christ's coming as the consummation of the age, the goal of the church, the crowning of Christ himself, the only hope of the world's redemption.

A. B. Simpson tells his readers of having visited a cathedral in Europe, upon the ceiling of which a famous painter of the past had patiently employed his brush. Upon entering the building his eyes sought the ceiling, and he saw what seemed a bewildering daubing of incoherent color. He looked long and earnestly; not a figure appeared; not a design was evident. The old sexton was passing about, and the visitor expressed to him his disappointment, whereupon he smiled and said: "No wonder, sir. You have no fit position from which to see this work of art. Come with me." And he led him to a place in the cathedral where the artist had evidently stood and bethought his designs, and to which he must have returned again and again as he wrought them into being. And lo, the visitor saw such a masterpiece as to bedim his eyes with tears and bow his head in gratitude to the God who had granted to one of his fellow servants such genius. Simpson reasons that what that position was to the study of the fresco painting, the premillennial position is to the understanding of the Word of God. It was the position of Ellicott, Tregelles, Godet, Stier, Delitzsch, Lange, Olshausen, DeWette, Meyer, Jamieson, Fausset, Schall, Bengel, Canon Ryle.

It was the position of Candlish and Guthrie; of Robert West, Robert Murray McCheyne and Adolph Saphir; of Gaussen, Van Oosterzee, Auberlen, Baumgarten; of Hoffmann, Stockmeyer, and Schenkel. It was the position of Spurgeon, Moody, Brookes, Moorehead, Gordon, and Blackstone; of Pierson and Penn. It is that of Meyer and Morgan; of Munhall and Chapman; of Haldeman and Dixon; of Torrey, Scofield, and Gaebelein.

In the language of Paul to the Hebrews, "What shall I say more; the time would fail me to tell of" Craven, Patterson, Erdman, and Dunwiddy; of Maitland, Birkes, Bickersteth, and Brock; of McNeile, McNeill, and MacNeil; of McIllvaine and Henshaw, Nicholson and Hastings; of the Robertsons, Frederick W. and John; of Saunders and Harris and Evans and Stifler; of Lorimer, Peters, and Durbin; of Parker, Gilbert, Foster, and Lummis, not to make mention of those men so well known to us that we do not yet appreciate their greatness: Frank W. Sneed, D. D. Munro, Frederick W. Farr, A. J. Frost, Len G. Broughton, W. B. Hinson, George Robert Cairns.

Moreover, some of the best preachers, pastors now of some of the greatest churches, are advocates of the personal, bodily, visible, imminent, triumphant, premillennial return of the risen, ascended Lord. These men believe, and scripturally so, that a preacher only half preaches the first coming of Christ if he neglects or ignores the second coming. It is like a preacher getting half through his sermon—then quitting.

Concerning Conditions

2 Timothy 3:1-13 speaks of the signs that immediately precede Christ's second coming and the conditions existent just before he returns:

1. "Men shall be lovers of their own selves" (v. 2)—the sign of abounding *selfishness.*

2. Men shall be "covetous" (v. 2)—the sign of inordinate *love of money.*

3. Men shall be "boasters, proud, . . . heady, highminded" (vv. 2-4)—the sign of human *haughtiness and pride.*

4. Men shall be "blasphemers, . . . unholy" (v. 2)—the sign of *disrespect for sacred things.*

5. Men shall be "disobedient to parents" (v. 2)—the sign of *disrespect to parental authority.*

6. Men shall be "unthankful" (v. 2)—the sign of *unthankfulness.*

7. Men shall be "without natural affection" (v. 3)—the sign of *hardness of heart.*

8. Men shall be "false accusers, . . . traitors" (vv. 3-4)—the sign of *disloyalty* to normal human obligations, as to friends, home, country.

9. Men shall be "incontinent, . . . led away with divers lusts" (vv. 3-6)—the sign of *sexual excesses and abuses.*

10. Men shall be "fierce" (v. 3)—the sign of brutality.

11. Men shall be "despisers of those that are good, . . . all that will live godly in Christ Jesus shall suffer persecution" (vv. 3-12)—the sign of *hatred and persecution* of godly people.

12. Men shall be "lovers of pleasure more than lovers of God" (v. 4)—the sign of excessive *pursuit of pleasure.*

13. Men shall have "a form of godliness, but denying the power thereof" (v. 5)—the sign of dead *religious formalism.*

14. Men shall be "ever learning, and never able to come to the knowledge of the truth" (v. 7)—the sign of *seeking religion, but denying revelation.*

15. Men shall be like Jannes and Jambres who withstood Moses (v. 8)—the sign of seeking to *oppose the truth* by presenting a clever but worthless imitation. Jannes and Jambres imitated Moses' miracle of the rod (Ex. 7:10-12).

16. Men shall be evil "and seducers [imposters] shall wax worse and worse, deceiving, and being deceived" (v. 13)—the sign of presenting a counterfeit Christianity. The exponents of this counterfeit Christianity will be men of corrupt minds, reprobate concerning the faith (v. 8).

Concerning Confusion

There will be confusion of face and terror of heart for those who are not ready for that great and glorious day of the Lord —the Watchman's looked-for day, the Purchaser's redemption day, the Builder's completion day, the Husbandman's harvest day, the Master's rewarding day, the Servant's reckoning day, the Son's manifestation day, the Bride's wedding day, the King's coronation day.

All who are not ready for that day will be in shame, and confusion will cover them. For all unbelievers there will be confusion of face and tormenting fear:

when the Lord Jesus shall be revealed from heaven with his mighty angels, In flaming fire taking vengeance on them that know not God, and that obey not the gospel of our Lord Jesus Christ: Who shall be punished with everlasting destruction from the presence of the Lord, and from the glory of his power; When he shall come to be glorified in his saints, and to be admired in all them that believe" (2 Thess. 1:7-10).

Paul talks of "that blessed hope, and the glorious appearing of the great God and our Saviour Jesus Christ" (Titus 2:13).

And John says: "Every man that hath this hope in him purifieth himself" (1 John 3:3).

John also urged readiness in these words: "Now, little children, abide in him; that, when he shall appear, we may have
confidence, and not be ashamed before him at his coming"
(1 John 2:28).

Jesus said: "Blessed are those servants, whom the Lord when
he cometh shall find watching" (Luke 12:37). "Watch . . .
for ye know neither the day nor the hour wherein the Son of
man cometh" (Matt. 25:13).

So the question we should answer, in the light of the certainty and suddenness of his coming, is: Are we ready? If you
are ready and you die before he comes, it means for you the
bursting of the bars of death on the day of the first resurrection. If you are alive and a Christian, it will mean for you that
glorious change in a moment.

If you are not a Christian and are dead when he comes, it
will mean for you one thousand years more in the grave until
the time when you come forth to the resurrection of dam-
nation. If you are not a Christian and are alive when he comes,
God only knows how terrible your plight when "one shall be
taken and the other left."

Biederwolf refers to the siege of Lucknow as one of the
thrilling episodes of English history. A small army of English
soldiers were in the garrison when it was surrounded by a
band of thirty thousand bloodthirsty savages crying for
vengeance and filling the air with war cries and terrifying
shrieks. By the aid of some trickery and skilful maneuvering
the English managed to slip quietly away. But one of their
number was left behind. When his companions stole away, he
was busy elsewhere. When he discovered his horrible plight,
he found himself alone in the garrison with thirty thousand
ferocious savages yelling for the sight of a white man's face
and for the taste of a white man's blood. But he, too, man-

aged to get away. When he caught up at last with his fleeing companions his hair had turned white with fright. When they asked him for his name, it had gone from his mind, and he did not know. He had been left behind. "Then shall two be in the field; the one shall be taken, and the other left. Two women shall be grinding at the mill; the one shall be taken, and the other left" (Matt. 24:40-41).

O God, make us wise to be ready for the day when the unbelieving world shall look on him whom they have pierced, and the redeemed of God shall be with him and in his safekeeping forevermore.

5

The Christian
Sense of the Future

CARL F. H. HENRY

HOPE in the future lends such meaning to life that even where the Christian revelation is unknown, men and women dream of some new era of promise. Many of the ancient religions and cults expectantly anticipated the future, as also did the poets of mythology with their solar immortalities. Present culture has its utopias, too, most of them secular revisions of an erstwhile spiritual concept.

Western scientism and Marxist communism have stripped all supernatural features from the vision of a coming kingdom, have linked it exclusively to the forces of nature and history, and have promised modern man an earthly paradise of material prosperity and security. Thus, confidence, either in forces supposedly immanent in nature and history or in man's ability to exploit such forces, has become the foundation of this era's hope for meaningful survival and destiny.

Importance of the Future

That the present is shaped by the future and not simply by the past has always, if rightly understood, been a major theme in biblical religion. As J. A. T. Robinson has said, because God's sovereignty extends into the remote future, "every statement about God is *ipso facto* an assertion about the end."[1] The future is not merely the realm of natural possibilities awaiting human actualization, nor is it a package of unforeseeable creativities latent in the *elan vital*. The future, rather, is what God's providential decree has in store for those who are made in his image.

The end toward which human life moves in its transition from the yesterdays to a new tomorrow is neither a perpetual dying in every present, nor final nothingness, nor need it be the sinner's condemnation to endless doom and eternal separation from the Holy Lord of all. What brightened the dark days of Jesus' persecuted followers was their radiant hope of the Lord's return in the final crisis and climax of history, their assurance that death means personal reunion with their crucified and risen Saviour, their unshakable conviction of righteousness' ultimate triumph and of evil's consignment to the darkest hell.

To recover the biblical perspective of last things—of "eschatology," to use the theological term—we shall need to question the attitude of some ministers today toward prophetic themes. For one thing, we must decry the neglect of eschatological themes by liberal Protestants. Thereby they reveal their uncertainty about God's transcendence over history and, consequently, their disbelief in the future supernatural fulfillment of the goal of history. In a word, liberal Protestantism lacks apocalyptic anticipation. Modernists dismissed the second advent of Christ as a distraction from the spiritual potentialities of the present world process—be it a dividend of Christ's first advent or an assured hope of Darwin's evolutionary premises.

---

[1] *In the End, God* (London: James Clarke & Co., 1950), p. 36.

At the 1955 assembly of the World Council of Churches in Evanston, however, European theologians challenged prevailing disinterest in eschatology. Since then Protestant theology has given increasing attention to the theme of the Christian hope. There is greater recognition today that eschatology cannot be dismissed as a pagan import into Hebrew-Christian religion. More and more acknowledge that the prophetic element is integral to the scriptural revelation, and that any "new order" projected by totalitarian dictators like Hitler and Khrushchev must come to terms with the "new age" already inaugurated by Jesus Christ.

Even this gain for biblical theology, however, is often obscured by "existential" speculations in which historical or objective aspects of prophecy are whittled to mere religious psychology or subjective response. If eschatological truth is just an invisible spiritual breeze that blows from somewhere into the sensitive souls of devout men and gives them courage to face the unpredictable future (which they alone can shape by courageous decision), then the biblical concept of end time has been largely dissolved. The study of prophecy must not deal exclusively with the future. Continuity prevails between the spiritual experience of the church through the ages and the coming last events.

The early church knew that Jesus' incarnation, death, and resurrection in some sense set "the last days" in motion (Acts 2:17; 2 Tim. 3:1; Heb. 1:2; 1 Pet. 1:20; 1 John 2:18). Since the risen Christ is head of the body of regenerate believers, all who are united to him by faith have in some vital way passed through death and judgment and are already now participating in some of the spiritual realities of a resurrection life. Of their inheritance of those powers and blessings peculiar to the age to come they enjoy a "sample" here on earth. Hence, the great realities of the Christian hope nourish the ethical dynamic of Christian life in this present age by enlivening the believer's attitudes and deeds, by quickening his missionary interest and responsibility.

But the future elements of the New Testament hope are far more than visual symbols of the final triumph of the believer's faith or existentialized dramatizations of the believer's "new being" in Christ. Whatever anticipations of the end time may inhere in the spiritual experience of Christians, at the close of history the Lord Jesus Christ will impinge upon the present personally and transcendently. Inaugurated by the coming of the Messiah, the Christian era fulfils the past Judaic era of promise, thereby instituting "the last days" and in some respects overlapping the prophetic end time. The present age is nonetheless intermediate, for even in its present sampling of certain features of the time to come it awaits the final and full consummation of all things.

Need for Biblical Balance

The expansion of eschatological concern has been encouraged in our own generation by the military threat of nuclear destruction, the rise of totalitarian political powers, the severe persecution and containment of Christians in Communist lands, and sometimes by the simple longing for security in an explosive world. More significant than all these factors, however, is the feeling for eschatological realities promoted by the noticeable recovery of interest in biblical theology.

Neglect of eschatological themes nevertheless still marks the preaching of many American clergymen. According to a survey of Protestant ministers by *Christianity Today*, only 30 per cent of the liberal and 26 per cent of the neo-orthodox clergy consider the second coming of Christ an essential doctrine in preaching, as contrasted with 93 per cent of the fundamentalist and 76 per cent of the conservative (but nonfundamentalist) clergy. If these findings are a reliable indication of ministerial attitudes as a whole, almost 50,000 American ministers, or one in four, feel no spiritual compunction whatever for reminding their congregations that the climax of history will be the personal, visible return of Jesus Christ in power and judgment. *Life* magazine's sampling of opinion at the Evanston assembly of the World Council showed that only 10 per cent of the American Protestant clergy find any significance in the doctrine of the second advent.

The axis of all New Testament eschatology is the second advent of Christ. While fundamentalist ministers emphasize the doctrine, they often create problems by placing the second coming in the wrong eschatological perspective. Not a few fundamentalists, unfortunately, (particularly extreme dispensationalists) become overly preoccupied with such secondary factors as the premillennial kingdom or the pre-tribulation rapture. When theological discussion concentrates on debatable issues—even when these are legitimate in proper perspective—it almost inevitably neglects or distorts the primary concerns of eschatology.

Lack of expository balance among some "prophetic teachers" has, in fact, disposed certain groups against any pursuit whatever of eschatological themes. Expositors of biblical prophecy are more cautious than they were two or three decades ago about identifying antichrists. The main stock in trade of some of these prophetic "specialists," however, often detours people far from the major eschatological avenues of apostolic thought.

The Triumph of Christ

Just as the Messiah's first advent was the key that gloriously unlocked the Christian era, so the Messiah's expected return is the prophetic sun around which revolves the consummation of the age of grace. The second coming of Christ is the one event in the future that is more certain than physical death.

Eschatology finds its true focus, then, in the *who* and *why* of the end time more than in the *when* and *where* and *what*. That is, every facet of the doctrine of last things magnifies Christ Jesus. The New Testament speaks of what precedes, accompanies, and follows the coming of the Lord. Wars, calamities, natural disorders, and political deceptions will prevail prior to his coming. Simultaneous with his coming, the present world order will be brought to an end. After his coming will appear the new heaven and new earth.

To what events does the New Testament give priority in expounding the second advent? In connection with the personal, visible return of Jesus Christ it speaks also of the conforming of believers to the image of the Redeemer: man will be restored to the original destiny that was his by creation. Although man forfeited his unique relationship to God by the fall, Christ's return will transform him to the full glory of the new humanity mirrored by the Saviour in the days of his flesh. At that day man will be fully sanctified by the Spirit who in this fleeting present age ministers the holy virtues of eternity to erase the sins of these earth-bound years. Only the return of the Redeemer can fulfil this glorious destiny of a redeemed humanity. It is in this context that the Christian pulpit is to proclaim the church's blessed hope. Prophetic proclamation not only stirs the unsaved by threatening the certainty of future judgment but, by emphasizing the radiant prospect and remarkable privileges of all Christ's followers, also scores the danger and tragedy of neglecting present opportunities of glory.

Besides the Lord's return for and with his saints, the New Testament exposition of last things includes also the resurrection of the body. In eternity the Redeemer's reconciliation will overrule the sundered selfhood of all men. All impenitent sinners, however, will be shut out from the Father's presence forever. The New Testament affirms the final judgment of all, each one's eternal destiny having been sealed by personal decision in this life prior to physical death.

The New Testament also intimates the ultimate triumph of Christ's redemptive work in history. A historical fall and consequently a historical triumph over the power and consequences of sin seem integral to the Christian revelation of redemption. Scripture gives no latitude, however, to misinterpret the triumph of grace in a universalistic direction.

Any proper exposition of the Christian concept of the future will take full note of the interrelationship between the biblical view of history and of the consummation of all things. While the Christian believer has a lively sense of future climax, he also lives day by day in the midst of the unfolding future.

The Christian knows that historical process has *purpose* (the redemptive initiative of the Creator-Redeemer-Judge constitutes its real plot) and that history has a *goal* (the complete end time vindication of the righteousness of God). As Leonard Hodgson reminds us in his Gifford Lectures, the biblical view of history is both teleological and eschatological; it affirms, that is, that the time-space universe expresses God's purposive will and also anticipates its final consummation. Jesus Christ is the central character in this great drama of redemptive history: in his first coming he supplied the ground of reconciliation; in his second coming he is pledged to consummate all the promises and judgments of God. The Jews looked forward to an *eschaton*, that conclusion of the historical time-series which was fully to reveal God's perfect kingdom as the underlying *telos* of history. The messianic manifestation in Christ defines two movements in the progress of redemptive revelation; it distinguishes, as it were, "the last days" from "the last day." As a revelation of God's will in sacred history, the coming of Jesus Christ, in Professor Hodgson's words, is "at once the *eschaton* of all that went before and the *proton* of all subsequent history."[2] While the new age has already come, the age to come still remains, when Christ in his *parousia* returns in power and glory.

The second advent of Christ, therefore, becomes the hub around which range the several spokes of the eschatological future: the resurrection of the dead, the final judgment, the reward of the righteous, the doom of the wicked. The New Testament doctrine of last things, therefore, affirms much more than faith in the future of the world and in human history under God. Its teaching cannot be reduced to the mere form of thought and language by which the biblical writers state their faith in God's sovereignty over history and in history's transcendent meaning. The biblical writers do, indeed, insist that the end of history is meaningfulness and fulfilment (not nothingness and frustration), that Antichrist can never overthrow the victory of truth and right, and that the last trump will announce not the fact of global destruction but the crowning kingdom of God.

Even the reference in Peter's epistles to the dissolution of the elements by fervent heat is set in the context of divine determination, not amid lurid predictions of a nuclear holocaust as popularized since Hiroshima and Nagasaki. What God began he will also complete; his purposes for man as revealed in Jesus Christ shall finally triumph. The Christian doctrine of hope is more than a redemptive view; it looks to redemptive deeds, to specific events, to climactic and crowning developments that embrace the personal destiny of the human race and the cosmic destiny of all creation.

God's Coming Judgment

This redemptive climax of history has far-reaching implications for the present debate over the meaning of life. The

---

[2]*For Faith and Freedom* (New York: Charles Scribner's Sons, 1957), p. 178.

Christian view does not hold that every deed of man is divinely effected and divinely approved. No wonder Karl Marx, looking at the social evils of his times, revolted against this so-called Christian view of his teacher in his university classes in Germany. "Whatever man is doing, God is doing," had been espoused by Hegel, the great liberal Protestant philosopher. On Hegel's pantheistic premises evil was nothing more than a finite illusion. Marx's revolt against Christianity as Hegel expounded it is, therefore, quite understandable. For in respect to the terrible reality of evil in this world, the God of the Bible is surely more on Marx's side than on Hegel's.

In revolting against liberal Protestant immanence, Marx regrettably moved to a nonsupernaturalistic view of history and spurned the God of the Bible and divine redemption from sin. According to the Christian view of history, all events are redeemable: God provides redemption for sinful men in specific saving events that work out his holy purpose in the full length of history. In a word, the solution of the problem of evil lies in God's true grace in history.

The sense in which communism is to be regarded as divine punishment, thus as a judgment of God upon the Western world, is seldom represented adequately. Unfortunately, it was a dull conscience in the face of social evils that provoked the Marxian reaction to radical views of property—views as erroneous, however, as the worst that Marx sought to correct. This radicalism, this repudiation of property rights, this insensitivity to divinely sanctioned rights and duties, it should be noted, arose in the context of liberal Protestantism which misrepresented the fallen social order as a part of the very life of the absolute (hence in no sense under divine judgment), as well as in a time of evangelical indifference toward social injustices. Communism should be recognized then, not only as a punishment of the West for its materialistic vices, but for its theological deformity as well.

More can be said on this point of theological penalty. Much of communism's vitality comes from copying, but profoundly perverting, Christian motifs. "Redemption" (Communists do not know the true meaning of the term) depends upon the activity of a "redeemer," a dialectic which rises above history and sweeps on toward a final day of victory. Mighty forces transcending the immanent laws of the historical process and the idea of a future kingdom of justice are concepts that Marxism borrowed at a distance from the Christian point of view and in a secular form turned against biblical Christianity. While the rise of communism cannot be considered as good or creative, it must nonetheless be viewed as an instrument of divine punishment. It signifies God's angry judgment, not only on contemporary history, but on much that has passed for Christianity in our times.

This comprehension provides a fuller insight into the ultimate significance of communism than the Marxists themselves possess. Those who imply by their appeal for "a sense of history" that the Communist thrust is one which the world can no longer reverse, would seem to presuppose a feeling of historical inevitability that must warm a Marxist heart. While modern man in himself may not be able to erase the Communist thrust, the work of a saving God can and will bring it under the same judgment that has toppled every other reliance upon man-made power.

The only hope that will endure the judgment of eternity is one which recovers the biblical view of history and trusts in its true Lord. Today the intermediate and cursory hopes of men are being measured and weighed by an everlasting hope that endures. "I thank God I have no provisional hopes," said a student in East Germany. "When I stand on the platform in a mass meeting of the Free German Youth to answer charges, I don't want to hope any more that I may be able to finish my course of study, or even that I may survive that meeting. I only hope that I may speak the truth and bear witness to the lordship and coming of Christ."[3]

In the aftermath of the world wars and in the face of the Sino-Soviet menace the Free World's utopian expectations have foundered and collapsed. Its spirit of questioning pessimism contrasts strangely with the millennial vision (understood as the triumph of the proletariat) aglow in some quarters of the Communist world. In addition to probings of the future by secular thinkers, the Christian community is showing new interest in the nature of Christ's final victory and his full vindication of righteousness. This growing recognition that the triumph of righteousness and grace is assured only on Christian premises, that is, in terms of *Jesus the World's Perfector* (as a recent book by Karl Heim is called), marks a happy turn in contemporary theological thought.

Unfortunately, however, this theme is often expounded on universalistic presuppositions. As a result, the vitality of the biblical doctrine of judgment and the urgency of personal acceptance of Christ in this life are dissipated at a time when world affairs, more than ever before, demand their uncompromised proclamation. For all its repudiation of Protestant modernism, the theology of Karl Barth nonetheless retains the modernist openness to universalism. While he does not commit himself to a universalistic conclusion, Barth's premise that all men are already embraced in Christ as God's elect and need only to be informed of this fact leads toward universalism.

Anglo-Saxon theologians tend to buttress the theory of universal salvation by appealing to their reconstructed concept of the nature of God, which subordinates righteousness and justice to love as the central core of divine life.

The Bible forthrightly teaches that at his second advent

---

[3] Charles C. West, *Communism and the Theologians* (Philadelphia: The Westminster Press, 1958), p. 284.

Jesus will openly take control of the world and achieve its final settlement and perfecting. This final phase of his messianic work involves the full, universal display of his "all power . . . in heaven and earth." Will "all men" automatically then begin a new life of communion with God? In discussing this question, Karl Heim in *Jesus the World's Perfector* pointedly refers us to Jesus' own intimations and declarations that all who reject Christ in this life are doomed to divine wrath in the life to come.

The church, as Leonard Hodgson reminds us, lives today "in the period between the time when Christ 'for us men and our salvation . . . was made man' and the time when He 'shall come with glory to judge both the quick and the dead,' " in a time "pregnant with meaning for action."⁴ Dr. Hodgson recalls a comment by R. H. Lightfoot:

> The life of the Church was to fill something more than a brief pause between the penultimate and the final scene. . . . The growth and experience of the Church had shown that the Lord's life was not only an event in Jewish history, but in world history. . . . It was itself the manifestation in history of the spiritual Power through which the worlds were made.

In these days the totalitarian "builders of new worlds" spring not from pagan countries (as did Genghis Khan, Hannibal, Tiglath-pileser); rather the Hitlers and Mussolinis and Khrushchevs rise from lands where the gospel has long been known. Perhaps the church is not far removed from the return and reign of him who, since his resurrection, has remained incognito before the world. If so, the bold proclamation of the evangel devolves as a duty upon us with the same urgency mirrored in the Acts of the Apostles. When he comes again,

---

⁴*Op. cit.*, p. 186.

he comes—as the Apostles' Creed succinctly announces—"to judge the quick and the dead." Never has the sure voice of winsome warning and witness been more imperative than now.

6
The Second Coming— a Practical Doctrine

J. D. GREY

IN Titus 2:11-15 Paul discusses briefly the doctrine of the second coming of Christ. Writing under divine inspiration, in the thirteenth verse he refers to this doctrine as "that blessed hope." This thought, as regards the second coming of Christ, is set forth in other places in the New Testament. Paul discusses this doctrine in 1 Thessalonians 4. In concluding the discussion, he says, "Wherefore comfort one another with these words" (v. 18). No greater hope can be given to the Christian to which he may hold in life's darkest hour than "that blessed hope, and the glorious appearing of the great God and our Saviour Jesus Christ" (Titus 2:13).

Titus 2:15 presents a positive command to ministers of the gospel to preach the second coming of Christ. It says, "These things speak, and exhort, and rebuke with all authority. Let no man despise thee." A minister of the gospel who never preaches on the second coming of Christ is not making full proof of his ministry. If he pleads that people are not interested in the subject, he should try preaching on it once to see how people will flock to hear him. If he pleads that he does not know anything about the doctrine, he should be ashamed of himself, search the Scriptures, and acquaint himself with the teaching regarding this blessed hope.

Sometimes the church is found holding to the false hope of converting the whole world. Frequently one hears ministers and other Christians speaking of "winning the world to Christ." Every now and then people are admonished to go forth and win the world. But as honest and as sincere as these persons who thus speak may be, the fact remains that nowhere did the Lord tell his disciples to win the world. He said, "Ye shall be witnesses unto me," in all parts of the world. He taught us to lead individuals, as such, throughout the world to a saving knowledge of him. But never did he say that we were to win the world to him. He who holds to the hope of converting the world is running after a mere phantom.

Another false hope of the church is that of overcoming the world in the sense of righting all the wrong, correcting all the faults, and curing all the ills. Jesus did tell us, as individuals, to overcome the world. 1 John 5:4 says, "This is the victory that overcometh the world, even our faith"—but remember the writer was speaking here to individuals concerning their relationship to the world of sin about them, instead of the church's being able to overcome the world. On the contrary, more often the world overcomes the church. God looks upon the world as a sinking ship. Men do not rush out to repaint and redecorate a sinking vessel. They simply seek to rescue those individuals who are aboard.

In 1 John 2:16-17, the world is analyzed in the following words: "For all that is in the world, the lust of the flesh, and the lust of the eyes, and the pride of life, is not of the Father, but is of the world. And the world passeth away, and the lust thereof: but he that doeth the will of God abideth forever."

We should try to apply the gospel to all areas of life, to be sure, but the return of Christ is the world's only hope. Following the Lord's teachings in all segments of society, we can improve the lot of many unfortunates. But the world order or this age of godlessness can never be perfected apart from the personal coming of Jesus Christ.

When one thinks of the doctrine of the "blessed hope," this doctrine of the second coming of Christ, he thinks immediately of the admonition given in the Scriptures which urges God's children to watchfulness in view of Christ's coming. Many good people have steered clear of discussing the blessed hope because a few have become fanatical on the subject and have reduced it to nothing more than a juggling of Scripture verses, figures, and dates. But even though there are many who, in thinking of this doctrine, have no more lofty purpose than that, you and I should not be kept from it, for it is a great doctrine. It is not only the blessed hope to bring comfort to our hearts but, viewed from every angle, the second coming of Christ is a practical doctrine.

It is practical in the first place because it arouses the saved. By the promise of his coming, the Lord urged the disciples to be watchful. He said in Matthew 24:42, "Watch therefore: for ye know not what hour your Lord doth come." The same admonition is found in Mark 13:34-37:

The Son of man is as a man taking a far journey, who left his house, and gave authority to his servants, and to every man his work, and commanded the porter to watch. Watch ye therefore: for ye know not when the master of the house cometh, at even, or at midnight, or at the cockcrowing, or in the morning: Lest coming suddenly he find you sleeping. And what I say unto you I say unto all, Watch.

He further urges his disciples in all ages to watchfulness by his words in Luke 12:35-38:

Let your loins be girded about, and your lights burning; and ye yourselves like unto men that wait for their lord, when he will return from the wedding; that when he cometh and knocketh, they may open unto him immediately. Blessed are those servants, whom the Lord when he cometh shall find watching: verily I say unto you, that he shall gird himself, and make them to sit down to meat, and will come forth and serve them. And if he shall come in the second watch, or come in the third watch, and find them so, blessed are those servants.

John in his Patmos vision saw the Lord at that time and heard him give this admonition to watchfulness: "Behold, I come as a thief. Blessed is he that watcheth, and keepeth his garments" (Rev. 16:15).

This doctrine also arouses the saved to sobriety. It calls them forth to live useful, sober lives for the Lord Jesus Christ. Paul urges us in 1 Thessalonians 5:6 to "not sleep, as do others; but let us watch and be sober." We find the same admonition given by the apostle Peter. In 1 Peter 1:13, he says, "Wherefore gird up the loins of your mind, be sober, and hope to the end for the grace that is to be brought unto you at the revelation of Jesus Christ." He also said, "But the end of all things is at hand: be ye therefore sober, and watch unto prayer" (1 Peter 4:7).

By this doctrine of the second coming, the saved are aroused to fidelity to the Lord. We do not know when he is coming, but we are urged to be found faithful to him when he does come. In Luke 12:42-44, the Lord tells us to be faithful:

The Lord said, Who then is that faithful and wise steward, whom his lord shall make ruler over his household, to give them their portion of meat in due season? Blessed is that servant, whom his lord when he cometh shall find so doing. Of a truth I say unto you, that he will make him ruler over all that he hath.

In Luke 19, Jesus gave the parable of the nobleman and the ten pounds as he said, "A certain nobleman went into a far country to receive for himself a kingdom, and to return. And he called his ten servants and delivered them ten pounds, and said unto them, Occupy till I come" (vv. 12-13). These are the words the Master would give to you and to me today. He wants every child of his to be faithful unto him and to watch for his return.

By the promise of his coming, we are admonished not to be ashamed of Christ in this world. For in Mark 8:38, he promises, "Whosoever therefore shall be ashamed of me and of my words in this adulterous and sinful generation; of him also shall the Son of man be ashamed, when he cometh in the glory of his Father with the holy angels."

This doctrine also arouses the saved against worldliness. When Christians are enticed by the allurement of the world, they should remember the words of the Master when he spoke of his second coming in Matthew 16:26-27: "What is a man profited, if he shall gain the whole world, and lose his own soul? or what shall a man give in exchange for his soul? For the Son of man shall come in the glory of his Father with his angels; and then he shall reward every man according to his works."

The apostle Paul uses the promise of the Lord's return as an incentive to mildness or moderation. In Philippians 4:5, he said, "Let your moderation be known unto all men. The Lord is at hand."

The promise of the return of Christ arouses the saved to patience. On this point, Hebrews 10:36-37 says, "Ye have need of patience, that, after ye have done the will of God, ye might receive the promise. For yet a little while, and he that shall come will come, and will not tarry." And in James 5:7-8, we read, "Be patient therefore, brethren, unto the coming of the Lord. Behold, the husbandman waiteth for the precious fruit of the earth, and hath long patience for it, until he receive the early and latter rain. Be ye also patient; stablish your hearts: for the coming of the Lord draweth nigh."

When Paul would urge Christians to mortify or kill fleshly lusts, he would do this by the promise of Christ's return. We hear him saying in Colossians 3:2-5:

Set your affection on things above, not on things on the earth. For ye are dead, and your life is hid with Christ in God. When Christ, who is our life, shall appear, then shall ye also appear with him in glory. Mortify therefore your members which are upon the earth; fornification, uncleanness, inordinate affection, evil concupiscence, and covetousness, which is idolatry.

By the promise of the second coming, the saved are aroused to live a life of sincerity. Paul, in his advice to the Philippians, wrote: "This I pray, that your love may abound yet more and more in knowledge and in all judgment; That ye may approve things that are excellent; that ye may be sincere and without offence till the day of Christ" (1:9-10).

Christians are urged to serve the Lord by loving the second coming of Christ. When Paul gave us the resume of his great and useful life, he told us in 2 Timothy 4:7-8 that: "I have fought a good fight, I have finished my course, I have kept the faith: Henceforth there is laid up for me a crown of righteousness, which the Lord, the righteous judge, shall give me at that day: and not to me only, but unto all them also that love his appearing." You and I will do well in this age in which we live to serve the Lord faithfully and love his appearing.

The saved are urged not only to love his appearing but to look for it and anxiously expect it. In Hebrews 9:27-28, we are admonished in the following words: "As it is appointed unto men once to die, but after this the judgment: So Christ was once offered to bear the sins of many; and unto them that look for him shall he appear the second time without sin unto salvation."

In the second place, the doctrine of the second coming of

Christ is practical in that it calls to consecration. Paul urges a practical dedication of our entire being: "The very God of peace sanctify you wholly; and I pray God your whole spirit and soul and body be preserved blameless unto the coming of our Lord Jesus Christ" (1 Thess. 5:23).

In the promise of Christ's return, we are urged to purify ourselves. As John said in his first epistle, "Beloved, now are we the sons of God, and it doth not yet appear what we shall be: but we know that, when he shall appear, we shall be like him; for we shall see him as he is. And every man that hath this hope in him purifieth himself, even as he is pure" (3:2-3).

John also urges us by the second coming to abide in Christ. He said, "Now, little children, abide in him; that, when he shall appear, we may have confidence, and not be ashamed before him at his coming" (1 John 2:28).

When Peter wanted to call us to consecration, to holy conversation and godliness, he spoke of Christ's return:

Seeing then that all these things shall be dissolved, what manner of persons ought ye to be in all holy conversation and godliness, Looking for and hasting unto the coming of the day of God, wherein the heavens being on fire shall be dissolved, and the elements shall melt with fervent heat? Nevertheless, we, according to his promise, look for new heavens and a new earth, wherein dwelleth righteousness (2 Peter 3:11-13).

In 1 Thessalonians 3:12-13 we are called to brotherly love by this doctrine in the following words of Paul: "The Lord make you to increase and abound in love one toward another, and toward all men, even as we do toward you: To the end he may stablish your hearts unblameable in holiness before God, even our Father, at the coming of our Lord Jesus Christ with all his saints."

Christians are called to separation from worldly lusts and to live godly lives by the thought of Christ's return:

The grace of God that bringeth salvation hath appeared to all men, Teaching us that, denying ungodliness and worldly lusts, we should live soberly, righteously, and godly, in this present world; Looking for that blessed hope, and the glorious appearing of the great God and our Saviour Jesus Christ (Titus 2:11-13).

We are urged to guard against hasty judgment. Paul said in 1 Corinthians 4:5, "Therefore judge nothing before the time, until the Lord come, who both will bring to light the hidden things of darkness, and will make manifest the counsels of the hearts: and then shall every man have praise of God."

When Paul urged the Christians at Corinth to a practical life of service, he let them know that faith in the second coming was a crowning grace and was an assurance that they would be blameless in the day of the Lord Jesus Christ. He said:

I thank my God always on your behalf, for the grace of God which is given you by Jesus Christ; that in every thing ye are enriched by him, in all utterance, and in all knowledge; even as the testimony of Christ was confirmed in you: So that ye come behind in no gift; waiting for the coming of our Lord Jesus Christ: Who shall also confirm you unto the end, that ye may be blameless in the day of our Lord Jesus Christ (1 Cor. 1:4-8).

Finally, we are called by the doctrine of the second coming of Christ to hold fast the hope which we have—firm to the end. When John was discouraged during his exile on lonely Patmos, the Lord would speak to encourage his heart. The word which was given to him was the promise that the Lord was soon coming back. In Revelation 2:25 he was told: "That which ye have already hold fast till I come." Also in Revelation 3:11 the Lord said to John, "Behold, I come quickly: hold that fast which thou hast, that no man take thy crown."

Therefore, as we study the Scriptures, we readily see that the doctrine of the second coming of Christ is not something over which we are to become fanatical. But it is, indeed, a practical doctrine by which we are urged—by which we urge others—to be watchful and to be ready for the Lord when he shall come back to this earth. Are you ready for him? If you are not, then get ready by yielding your heart and life completely to him.

7

"From Henceforth Expecting"

HERSCHEL H. HOBBS

"BUT this man, after he had offered one sacrifice for sins for ever, sat down on the right hand of God; from henceforth expecting till his enemies be made his footstool" (Heb. 10:12-13). When Jesus ascended into heaven it was with the promise that he would return. This second advent would be in great splendor, pomp, and power. That event is the "blessed hope, and [even] the glorious appearing of the great God and our Saviour Jesus Christ" (Titus 2:13). The promise is certain. The hope is sure.

But what of the interim between Jesus' ascension and second appearing? What is Jesus doing now? And what should we be doing meanwhile? These questions are of greater importance than the setting of dates or the plotting of events which may or may not herald the return of our Lord.

Where is Jesus now? The author of Hebrews tells us that he is seated on the right hand of God. That is the position of power. As he sits in this exalted place, what is he doing? Again this author says that he is "from henceforth expecting." Now what does he mean by this?

79

Examination of these words proves most rewarding. "From henceforth" translates two Greek words *(to loipon)* meaning "what remains, hereafter, for the future, henceforth." A. T. Robertson translates the words "for the rest" or "for the future." He calls it an accusative of the extent of time. This refers to the interval between the ascension and the second coming of Christ. Its length is of uncertain duration. Already it has extended for almost two thousand years. How much longer this will be no man can say.

"Expecting" is the participial form of a verb meaning "to look for, expect, wait for, await." In the present tense, as here, it expresses the continuing attitude of Jesus in this interim time.

So we see Jesus seated in the position of power and, for the period which separates his ascension and second advent, expecting. What is he expecting? Let us seek to answer this question as we note: (1) the success of the redemptive plan, (2) the fulfilment of the promise of God, and (3) the faithfulness of his people.

First, Jesus is expecting the success of the redemptive plan. When on the cross he cried, "It is finished" (John 19:30), he had completed God's will for his incarnation. Henceforth God will authenticate Jesus' work as he declares him to be "the Son of God with power . . . by the resurrection from the dead" (Rom. 1:4). The author of Hebrews emphasizes this as he quotes from Psalm 40:6-8.

Wherefore when he cometh into the world, he saith, Sacrifice and offering thou wouldest not, but a body hast thou prepared me: in burnt offerings and sacrifices for sin thou hast had no pleasure. Then said I, Lo, I come (in the volume [roll] of the book it is written of me,) to do thy will, O God (Heb. 10:5-7).

The animal sacrifices made under the law were insufficient for the redemption of man. For that reason God abrogated the old covenant that he might give a new one. The old covenant centered in the priest who "standeth daily ministering and offering oftentimes the same sacrifices, which can never take away sins" (v. 11). "But this man [this priest], after he had offered one sacrifice for sins for ever, sat down on the right hand of God; from henceforth expecting . . ." (vv. 12-13).

This suggests a glimpse at the actual manner of Jesus' death. The various Gospel accounts may differ in minor details, but they all agree that Jesus died a purposeful death. Mark and Luke simply state that he "gave up the ghost" or expired. Matthew says that he "dismissed" his spirit (author's translation). But John says much more. He says that Jesus himself "delivered" (author's translation) his spirit to God (John 19:30). Involved in the Greek word is the thought of delivering to someone something to keep, use, take care of, or manage (cf. Matt. 11:27; 25:14). The Father had "delivered" to the Son his redemptive purpose. Now the Son delivers his finished work back to the Father to keep, use, and manage.

This same thought is involved in Luke's statement—"Father, into thy hands I commend my spirit . . ." (23:46). The word "commend" translates a word meaning to place beside, near, or to set as food before one on the table (10:8). In the middle voice, as in Luke 23:46, it means to place down from one's self, to deposit, entrust, or to commit to one's charge (cf. 1 Tim. 1:18; 6:20; 2 Tim. 2:2). The idea is to give something over to another with the power to use it.

Thus, we see the Son seated at the right hand of God, having committed to the Father his redemptive work to be used in the salvation of a lost world. He is expecting that his once-for-all sacrifice (Heb. 9:28) shall suffice for the forgiveness of sins to all who believe in him.

This thought is involved in the words of Hebrews 10:12—"But this man [priest], after he had offered one sacrifice for sins for ever, sat down."

The contrast is between the priests of the old covenant who "standeth daily ministering and offering oftentimes the same sacrifices which can never take away sins" (Heb. 10:11) and the priest of the new covenant who offered one sacrifice forever. Henceforth he is seated in the attitude of a finished work. The Old Testament priests are never pictured as seated but always standing in the performance of an unfinished or futile ministry.

Now in this interim we are not to think of Jesus as inactive. For one thing, the first time anyone saw Jesus after the ascension he was "standing on the right hand of God" (Acts 7:56). This is not fanciful reasoning but the suggestion of the continuing concern that our Lord has for his own in their trials.

We see his activity more clearly perhaps as one who "ever liveth to make intercession for them" (Heb. 7:25). Elsewhere Jesus is spoken of as our advocate before the Father (1 John 2:1). These passages do not mean that God is praying to God. They merely suggest to us that the evidence of his sacrifice is ever before the Father as the surety that the price of man's redemption has been paid (Heb. 9:12, 24-28). Henceforth the issue rests with the response of man with regard to Jesus' redemptive work.

In that light Jesus is "from henceforth expecting"—expecting the Father to honor his promise to save all who believe on him. He is expecting those for whom he died to receive the redemption thus provided.

Second, Jesus is expecting the fulfilment of the promise of God. "From henceforth expecting till his enemies be made his footstool" (Heb. 10:13). This is an obvious reference to Psalm 110:1. There the psalmist says, "The Lord said unto my Lord, Sit thou at my right hand, until I make thine enemies thy footstool." Here we are given a glimpse into the eternal council before the foundation of the world, where the Father promised full and final victory to the Son over every kind of evil that opposes God. The author of Hebrews permits us to look beyond the ascension as we see the Son waiting expectantly for this promise to be fulfilled.

This picture is brought into clearer focus by Paul in 1 Corinthians 15:24-25. Here the apostle takes the fartherest view into the future of any writer in the New Testament. "Then [at the second coming of Christ] cometh the end, when he shall have delivered up the kingdom to God, even the Father; when he shall have put down all rule and all authority and power. For he must reign, till he hath put all enemies under his feet." Note that the two uses of the word "when" (*hotan*) refer not to time but to condition. It is the condition of the putting down of all forces that oppose God. This condition will make possible another in which the kingdom shall be handed over to the Father.

Examination of this statement by Paul is most revealing. The "end" referred to is not so much an element of time but of the goal of God's redemptive purpose which centers in a condition as seen above. The apostle says that "he must reign" until this condition obtains. Literally, "it is abidingly necessary, or binding upon him, to reign as a King" up to the point of the absolute subjection of all the enemies of God.

It is of interest at this point to ask as to when the reign of Christ begins. We believe that the burden of New Testament teaching is to the effect that he is reigning now. In 1 Corinthians 15:24 "shall have put down" is a constative aorist tense covering the entire period of conflict from the resurrection of Jesus until final and complete victory is achieved. The kingdom came when the King came (Matt. 3:2). In the disciples' skirmishes with evil Jesus saw the foretaste of the ultimate victory over Satan (Luke 10:18). In his death he engaged in mortal combat with Satan. Jesus was declared by the Father to be the Son of God with power because of his resurrection from the dead (Rom. 1:4). At the right hand of God he continues to reign until "he hath put all enemies under his feet" (1 Cor. 15:25). Thus, in the incarnation, we see the initial victory. The continuing conflict spans the period from the resurrection to the second coming. Final victory will then be achieved. Then the kingdom shall be delivered up to God, even the Father, "that God may be all in all" (v. 28).

All other words about the end time close with Jesus reigning supreme. But Paul takes a final glance through the curtain of mystery which separates time from eternity to see the Son delivering the subdued kingdom to the Father. Why? "When [condition] all things [the entire universe] shall be subdued unto him, then shall the Son also himself be subject unto him that put all things under him, that God may be all in all" (v. 28). The word "subdued" means to line up as a troop or an army in subordination or surrender. This verb appears three times in verse 28. Literally it reads, "Now when the universe shall be lined up as a troop in subordination to him, then also himself the Son shall be lined up as a troop in subordination to the One lining up a troop in subordination to him, in order that God may be all in all."

This is the most tremendous statement in the New Testament regarding the future in eternity. It visualizes the time when God shall be all in all. It does not mean that the Son and Holy Spirit shall cease to be. Rather it emphasizes the unity of God.

The Bible reveals God as one who reveals himself as Father, Son, and Holy Spirit. But this is due not to any weakness in God. It is the result of weakness in man. Finite man cannot comprehend an infinite God. Thus a redeeming God condescends to man's frailty by revealing himself as three persons involved in redemption. God the Father prepared redemption; God the Son provided it; God the Holy Spirit propagates it. But always it is God at work. Now when the redemptive purpose of God is complete, when all evil has been subdued, man will no longer need this threefold revelation. He shall see God as he is—a unity—that God may be all in all. It is a tremendous thought, but it is what Paul is saying.

So Jesus is expecting God to fulfil his promise to the end that he may present a subdued kingdom to the Father—that God may be all in all.

Third, Jesus is expecting the faithfulness of his people. In Hebrews 10 the author proceeds to mention the Holy Spirit as a witness to us regarding the redemptive work of Christ (v. 15). He then refers to the new covenant promised through Jeremiah (31:33) and given through Jesus (cf. Heb. 8:8-13). This covenant involves the priesthood of all believers. This priesthood is not only one of privilege (v. 10-11). It is also one of responsibility. In verse 10 the phrase "they shall be to me a people" reminds us of God's covenant with Israel (Ex. 19:1-6), whereby Israel was to be a priest nation endeavoring to bring all peoples to the true worship of Jehovah. When Israel failed to live up to that covenant, God instituted another through Jesus Christ. Henceforth his people are to be a priest people declaring the gospel of salvation to a lost world.

So Jesus is expecting us to be faithful to his commission and our trust. We believe this to be the theme of the entire book of Hebrews. The word "faith" or faithfulness is, perhaps, the key word of the book. It reaches its climax in chapter 11. After reciting the faithfulness of many in their generations, the author closes with these words: "These all, having obtained a good report through faith, received not the promise: God having provided some better thing for us, that they without us should not be made perfect" (vv.39-40). The word "perfect" implies a goal, and that goal is the full realization of the redemptive purpose of God. If we fail in our generation, then the eternal purpose of God (Eph. 3:11) will not be realized, at least through us. God's purpose will not fail. But, as in the case of Kadesh-barnea, it may be delayed for a generation. Therefore, these closing words in Hebrews 11 should be our watchword in missions and evangelism.

We are living in troublesome times. This could well be the last generation! But even if it is not, it is our only generation. Jesus taught that we should live in a state of constant expectancy with regard to his return.

A doctor friend of mine said, "I do not know when the Lord will return in final glory. But according to the tables of life expectancy I know that so far as my life is concerned, he will return for me within a very few years. Therefore, I must do all that I can for him now."

This should be the attitude of each of us. Our primary task is not to seek to chart the timetable, although it is most tempting to do so. Our responsibility is to prepare men's hearts for his return whenever it may be.

Yes, Jesus is expecting. How often we disappoint him! He has done all that he can do for the redemption of our race. Through the Holy Spirit working in us God would proclaim this message to all men. We often try to witness and fail. More often we fail because we do not try.

> The soul of Jesus is restless today;
> Christ is tramping through the spirit-world,
> Compassion in His heart for the fainting millions;
> He trudges through China, through Poland,
> Through Russia, Austria, Germany, Armenia;
> Patiently He pleads with the Church,
> Tenderly He woos her.
> The wounds of His body are bleeding
>   afresh for the sorrows of His shepherdless people.
> We besiege Him with selfish petitions,
> We weary Him with our petty ambitions,
> From the needy we bury Him in piles of carven stone,
> We obscure Him in the smoke of stuffy incense,
> We drown His voice with the snarls and shrieks of our
>   disgruntled bickerings,

We build temples to Him with hands that are bloody,
We deny Him in the needs and sorrows of the exploited—
    "least of His brethren."
The soul of Jesus is restless today,
But eternally undismayed.

CYPRUS R. MITCHELL

8

A Layman Looks at the Second Coming of Christ

L. NELSON BELL

THE fact of our Lord's return has too often been obscured by those who deny it, those who ignore it, and by those who set up a sequence of events having to do with his return and who argue for their particular viewpoint more than for the fact of his coming.

To deny that our Lord will return to this earth involves the denying of multiplied statements in the Scriptures which affirm the certainty of this event.

To ignore his return is to ignore one of the most important doctrines in all of the Bible and at the same time to miss the blessings which flow from this hope.

To becloud the issue by setting up a rigid schedule, some of which may be biblical but much of which is hypothetical, is to miss the wonder and anticipation of Christ's return and, at the same time, to repel many who otherwise might share in this anticipation.

It is tragic that the glory of our Lord's certain return has been tarnished by arguments about secondary matters and that it is a matter of record that some of the most ardent exponents of the second coming are deterrents to others who might believe. The fact, however, that those who persistently reject this truth often point to unsound arguments to bolster their position does not invalidate the truth itself.

There is a crying need for a clear, sane, and compelling witness to what the Bible teaches about the return of the Lord Jesus Christ to this earth. It is a frequently mentioned doctrine in the Bible. Wherever believed and acted upon on a scriptural basis, it brings blessing and clarification of thinking to individuals and to churches.

A study of what the Bible teaches about the second coming brings perspective out of chaos, hope out of gloom, and produces Christian action because of a resulting sense of responsibility.

Any consideration of the second coming of Christ demands a consideration of the Old Testament prophecies having to do with his first coming. Beginning in Genesis 3:15 and running through the entire Old Testament, there is the promise of a coming Redeemer. His name is given, his birthplace pinpointed, and his work described.

Believers such as Anna and Simeon, basing their faith on the Old Testament prophecies, recognized him and glorified God when they saw him in the Temple.

We find the Old Testament prophecies about the Messiah carried out in minute detail as our Lord's life and mission are unfolded in the New Testament. In all honesty we must, therefore, expect the same God who fulfilled his word about the advent of his Son into human history over nineteen hundred years ago to also fulfil all that he has promised about his return in power and great glory.

As the Old Testament ends with a warning, "Lest I come and smite the earth with a curse" (Mal. 4:6), so the New

Testament ends with the hope of his coming: "Surely I come quickly. Amen. Even so, come, Lord Jesus" (Rev. 22:20).

There is an inescapable sense of urgency in the world to-day. No longer can men lightly regard the signs of the times. On every hand things point to some kind of climax. What does the Bible say?

The Certainty of His Coming

If one is prepared to accept the clear and unequivocal statements of the Bible, he must be prepared to believe that Christ is certainly coming back.

Jesus, himself, said he will return.—Speaking to his confused and despondent disciples, he said: "If I go and prepare a place for you, I will come again, and receive you unto myself; that where I am, there ye may be also. I will not leave you comfortless: I will come to you" (John 14:3,18).

In the chapters in Matthew having to do with the Lord's return and the end of the age, we find such statements by our Saviour as the one in 26:64: "Hereafter shall ye see the Son of man sitting on the right hand of power, and coming in the clouds of heaven."

Again, we hear him saying (25:31): "When the Son of man shall come in his glory, and all the holy angels with him, then shall he sit upon the throne of his glory."

In Mark 14:62, we find our Lord affirming: "Ye shall see the Son of man sitting on the right hand of power, and coming in the clouds of heaven." In Luke 9:26, we read, "Whosoever shall be ashamed of me and of my words, of him shall the Son of man be ashamed, when he shall come in his own glory, and in his Father's, and of the holy angels."

Speaking of his return, our Lord further said:

As the days of Noe were, so shall also the coming of the Son of man be. For as in the days that were before the flood they were eating and drinking, marrying and giving in marriage, until the day that Noe entered into the ark, and knew not until the flood came, and took them all away; so shall also the coming of the Son of man be (Matthew 24:37-39).

On still another occasion, Matthew reports our Lord as saying: "The Son of man shall come in the glory of his Father with his angels; and then he shall reward every man according to his works" (16:27). And there are many other verses which could be cited to show the specific teaching of our Lord with reference to his return.

The Holy Spirit, speaking through the apostles, said that he will return.—Following the healing of the lame man at the gate of the Temple, Peter preached to the assembled multitude and, after exhorting them to repentance, added: "He shall send Jesus Christ, which before was preached unto you: Whom the heaven must receive until the times of restitution of all things, which God hath spoken by the mouth of all his holy prophets since the world began" (Acts 3:20-21).

Writing to the Corinthian Christians, Paul says: "So that ye come behind in no gift; waiting for the coming of our Lord Jesus Christ: Who shall also confirm you unto the end, that ye may be blameless in the day of our Lord Jesus Christ" (1 Cor. 1:7-8). Again, in the same letter, he says: "Judge nothing before the time, until the Lord come, who both will bring to light the hidden things of darkness, and will make manifest the counsels of the hearts" (4:5).

In telling of the revelation which he had from Jesus Christ that had to do with the institution of the Lord's Supper (1 Cor. 11:26), Paul goes on to say: "As often as ye eat this bread, and drink this cup, ye do shew the Lord's death till he come."

To the Philippian Christians he wrote: "Our conversation is in heaven; from whence also we look for the Saviour, the Lord Jesus Christ: Who shall change our vile body, that it may be fashioned like unto his glorious body, according to the working whereby he is able even to subdue all things unto himself" (3:20-21).

In Colossians 3:4 we read: "When Christ, who is our life, shall appear, then shall ye also appear with him in glory." In 1 Thessalonians 3:13 we find these words: "To the end he may stablish your hearts unblameable in holiness before God, even our Father, at the coming of our Lord Jesus Christ with all his saints." In this same epistle Paul further makes this affirmation: "The Lord himself shall descend from heaven with a shout, with the voice of the archangel, and with the trump of God: and the dead in Christ shall rise first" (4:16).

In 1 Thessalonians we also read:

Yourselves know perfectly that the day of the Lord so cometh as a thief in the night. For when they shall say, Peace and safety; then sudden destruction cometh upon them, as travail upon a woman with child; and they shall not escape. . . . I pray God your whole spirit and soul and body be preserved blameless unto the coming of our Lord Jesus Christ (5:2-23).

One of the most awesome statements having to do with our Lord's return is found in Paul's second letter to the Thessalonians:

To you who are troubled rest with us, when the Lord Jesus shall be revealed from heaven with his mighty angels, in flaming fire taking vengeance on them that know not God, and that obey not the gospel of our Lord Jesus Christ: Who shall be punished with everlasting destruction from the presence of the Lord, and from the glory of his power; when he shall come to be glorified in his saints, and to be admired in all them that believe (because our testimony among you was believed) in that day (1:7-10).

To Titus, Paul writes: "Looking for that blessed hope, and the glorious appearing of the great God and our Saviour Jesus Christ" (2:13).

The apostle James takes up the same refrain: "Be patient therefore, brethren, unto the coming of the Lord. . . . Be ye also patient; stablish your hearts: for the coming of the Lord draweth nigh, . . . behold, the judge standeth before the door" (5:7-9).

The apostle Peter frequently refers to the second coming of the Lord, giving us this clear prophecy: "But the day of the Lord will come as a thief in the night; in the which the heavens shall pass away with a great noise, and the elements shall melt with fervent heat, the earth also and the works that are therein shall be burned up" (2 Peter 3:10).

The same refrain is taken up by the aged apostle John: "Little children, abide in him; that, when he shall appear, we may have confidence, and not be ashamed before him at his coming" (1 John 2:28); and again: "But we know that, when he shall appear, we shall be like him; for we shall see him as he is" (3:2).

In Revelation John gives us a message straight from our Lord: "Behold, he cometh with clouds; and every eye shall see him, and they also which pierced him: and all kindreds of the earth shall wail because of him" (1:7).

Then in the final chapter of Revelation, these words: "Behold, I come quickly; and my reward is with me, to give every man according as his work shall be. He which testifieth these things saith, Surely I come quickly. Amen. Even so, come, Lord Jesus" (22:12,20).

The angels at his ascension said that he would return.—We know that the testimony of the angels at the time of our Lord's birth was true. We know that the testimony of the two men clothed in white at the tomb of the risen Lord was also true. Now we find the heavenly messengers saying, "This same Jesus, which is taken up from you into heaven, shall so come in like manner as ye have seen him go into heaven" (Acts 1:11).

These and many other verses affirm to us the certainty of our Lord's coming.

The Manner of His Coming

First of all, his coming will be *personal*. "The Lord himself shall descend from heaven" (1 Thess. 4:16).

In the second place, his return will be *bodily*, for in Acts 1:11 we are told, "This same Jesus, which is taken up from you into heaven, shall so come in like manner as ye have seen him go into heaven." The one who returns will be the risen Lord, with the scars in his hands and feet and in his side. It will be a bodily return.

In the third place, Jesus' return will be *visible*. "Behold, he cometh with clouds; and every eye shall see him" (Rev. 1:7).

One would be very dogmatic to assert that our Lord's return will be witnessed by worldwide television. Nevertheless, in the last few months Telstar has become indeed a reality, and the objection raised by some that "every eye shall see him" poses an insuperable question has now been removed at the merely scientific level.

His coming will be *unexpected* by many. "The day of the Lord will come as a thief in the night" (2 Peter 3:10). Unquestionably, just as in the days of Noah prior to the flood, many will hold up to derision the very thought of our Lord's return, so that for them his coming will be an unspeakable calamity.

Our Lord's return will be *catastrophic* for the unbeliever. Little wonder that we are told that a day is coming when men will seek to hide in the caves and will cry out to the mountains and the rocks to hide them from the presence of the Lord.

His coming will also be *sudden*. "As the lightning cometh out of the east, and shineth even unto the west; so shall also the coming of the Son of man be" (Matt. 24:27).

According to the Scriptures, then, the manner of Christ's

coming will be such that all men will grasp it with their natural senses: personal, bodily, visible, unexpected, catastrophic, and sudden.

The Purpose of His Coming

Our Lord will return to claim his own. When the shout of heaven will be heard with the voice of the archangel and with the trump of God, we are told, "The dead in Christ shall rise first: Then we which are alive and remain shall be caught up together with them in the clouds, to meet the Lord in the air: and so shall we ever be with the Lord" (1 Thess. 4:16-17).

Another purpose of his coming will be to institute judgment. Those who have rejected him, we are told, "shall be punished with everlasting destruction from the presence of the Lord, and from the glory of his power" (2 Thess. 1:9). Our Lord speaks of this time of judgment:

Then shall appear the sign of the Son of man in heaven: and then shall all the tribes of the earth mourn, and they shall see the Son of man coming in the clouds of heaven with power and great glory. . . . he shall send his angels with a great sound of a trumpet, and they shall gather together his elect from the four winds, from one end of heaven to the other (Matt. 24:30-31).

Behold, I come quickly; and my reward is with me, to give every man according as his work shall be (Rev. 22:12).

He will also come back to fulfil his promise. As he tells us in John 14:3, "If I go and prepare a place for you, I will come again, and receive you unto myself; that where I am, there ye may be also." And again, "Now I have told you before it come to pass, that, when it is come to pass, ye might believe" (v. 29).

He will also come to establish his kingdom. Because this will involve a new heaven and a new earth and because our present heaven and earth shall pass away, we are confronted with the mystery of the kingdom of God and the "holy city, new Jerusalem, coming down from God out of heaven, prepared as a bride adorned for her husband" (Rev. 21:2).

The redeemed will find themselves in an entirely new situation. "Behold, the tabernacle of God is with men, and he will dwell with them, and they shall be his people, and God himself shall be with them, and be their God" (v. 3). To dogmatize on this glorious truth can be very unprofitable. The reality and the glory are enough. We know that he shall reign and that we shall be with him for all eternity.

The Effect of This Anticipation

The prospect of our Lord's return—an event which may take place at any moment—should lead to personal godliness. Paul tells us in 1 Thessalonians 5:23, "I pray God your whole spirit and soul and body be preserved blameless unto the coming of our Lord Jesus Christ." In verse 8 we read, "But let us, who are of the day, be sober, putting on the breastplate of faith and love; and for an helmet, the hope of salvation." In speaking of this same hope, the apostle Peter says:

Seeing then that all these things shall be dissolved, what manner of persons ought ye to be in all holy conversation and godliness, looking for and hasting unto the coming of the day of God, . . . wherefore, beloved, seeing that ye look for such things, be diligent that ye may be found of him in peace, without spot and blameless (2 Peter 3:11-14).

There are many effects of a lively anticipation of the Lord's return. It should produce faithful stewardship, God-centered optimism, a proper perspective in our attitude to this world and the next, and a genuine zeal for evangelism and world missions. Our Lord said, "This gospel of the kingdom shall be preached in all the world for a witness unto all nations; and then shall the end come" (Matt. 24:14). This lays on Christians the clear responsibility to bear witness to the gospel message with unflagging zeal, knowing that in so doing they are hastening the coming of the Lord.

The Signs of His Coming

It is probable that Christians are often led to unwisely interpret world events, thinking that in them they see the personalities or incidents which indicate the Lord's immediate return. Many of us remember when Mussolini was proclaimed as the Antichrist—and then it was Hitler. We know that down through past history other individuals have been designated in like manner. Nevertheless, it is a fact that the coming of the Lord should not take believers entirely by surprise. In 1 Thessalonians 5:4-6, we read: "But ye, brethren, are not in darkness, that that day should overtake you as a thief. Ye are all the children of light, . . . Therefore let us not sleep, as do others; but let us watch and be sober."

There are many signs which may indicate the near coming of the Lord: the development of Israel as a separate nation; growing lawlessness in the world; men's longing for a world leader to bring "peace," which could well eventuate in the appearing of the Antichrist; the growing tendency toward a United States of Europe; the possibility that world business may be dominated and controlled in a completely arbitrary manner; and the obvious failure of man to solve his own problems. Couple all this with man's unwillingness to turn to the One who has the solution and who has offered it to all men who will believe—these and many other signs would certainly point to the possibility that the age is drawing to a close.

The Time of His Coming

For anyone to set a date for the returning of the Lord is utterly foolish, for this secret is locked in the counsels of eternity. God alone knows the time of Christ's return to this earth.

It has been argued that Paul thought the coming of the Lord was near and that he was mistaken. The simple fact is that with God a day is as a thousand years and a thousand years as a day. From the time of our Lord's ascension into heaven, his return has always been imminent. This will be true if another millennium goes by without his having come.

That which our Lord demands of his servants is that we shall be at all times watchful for his coming, knowing that it is certain and that it may be imminent.

There are some strange arguments against the second coming of the Lord. Some say that the time of his coming was at Pentecost, but let us remember that many of the predictions of our Lord's return were made after Pentecost.

There are many who say today that the spread of Christianity in the world is the second coming of Christ. But the spread of Christianity or the gospel witness throughout the world is a process, whereas the return of the Lord is a cataclysmic event.

There are also those who say that the Lord returns when we accept him as our Saviour. This act of accepting, however, is the entering into of a personal relationship with Jesus Christ, whereas the second coming of the Lord affects the entire world—either with unspeakable joy or abject terror.

As one reads the Old and new Testaments, he is impressed with the overwhelming fact that the Christ to whom was delegated the authority and power of creation, who came back into this world to redeem it from sin, is certainly coming back to judge and to reign.

This "day of the Lord," referred to by Peter, is a catastrophic event in which the fire of God's cleansing power is manifested in a way strangely like the devastating force of an atomic blast: "But the day of the Lord will come as a thief in the night; in the which the heavens shall pass away with a great noise, and the elements shall melt with fervent heat, the earth also and the works that are therein shall be burned up" (2 Peter 3:10).

This day is future, but it may come at any moment. It is a time when all men will be confronted with their own powerlessness in the presence of the sovereign God.

This will be a day of decisive and final action, a day of purification by fire. For the redeemed it will be a day of unspeakable joy; for those who have rejected him, one of utter catastrophe.

God in his goodness has told us of this coming day, and Peter says: "We have also a more sure word of prophecy; whereunto ye do well that ye take heed, as unto a light that shineth in a dark place, until the day dawn, and the day star arise in your hearts" (2 Peter 1:19).

The gospel message is one of God's offer of love and redemption to a lost and sinning world. To be true to the Scriptures, the gospel must be preached in the light of God's judgment. Everything centers around the cross of Calvary. On that cross we see the holiness, justice, and judgment of God combined in one sublime act with his love, mercy, and compassion.

We live today in what is spoken of as the "dispensation of grace," or the "era of the church." This is not an indefinite and unending period, however, but merely an interlude during which God in love and mercy and compassion is offering redemption to all who will accept him.

The curtain of history will be drawn by the Creator of time. All nations and men will stand before him, either with inexpressible joy or to be judged. Those who have accepted forgiveness and pardon through Jesus Christ have nothing to fear. Theirs is only glorious anticipation. For the Christian, the return of our Lord is truly "the blessed hope."

9
Revelation's Consummation

H. LEO EDDLEMAN

THE second coming of the Lord is to his first coming what Jesus' resurrection was to his death. Its relationship is one of climax to plot. It is to be the final of a long series of victories, interspersed with many apparent defeats. The resurrection climaxed his atoning death and proved the efficacy of his work on the cross. If the Lord had lain in the grave indefinitely after the crucifixion, we would never have known whether his death had dealt effectively with sin. Death is a chief fruit of sin. When he rose from the dead on the third day, it became evident that he had died a death that was victorious over sin. Thus his resurrection destroyed sin's chief fruit, and Christ lives on to perpetuate his saving ministry.

Similarly, the return of Christ to this earth to finish all that he "began both to do and teach" (Acts 1:1) is a necessary consummation to his total mission as Prophet, Priest, and King. Philosophically, it would be illogical for him not to come; theologically, it would be inconsistent for him not to come; historically, his work would be incomplete without his return.

The sudden, bodily appearance of Jesus Christ on earth's stage would seem fantastic. If accompanied by a cataclysmic consummation of history, the idea of his personal advent staggers the imagination. Yet, is it more "unnatural" than the first coming of Christ? Born of a virgin; bursting suddenly into Israelite history after following the laws of natural life three decades; three years and three months of startling teachings and miracles; a phenomenal death followed by a climactic resurrection—all seem more extraordinary on recalling that his post-resurrection appearances transformed cowardly men into courageous witnesses who lifted the stream of history out of its channel and redirected it.

Most Hebrews missed the glory of the first coming partly because it seemed too fantastic to be true. In spite of numerous prophecies specifying the place where Christ would be born, the facts concerning his virgin mother, meticulous descriptions of his death (Isa. 53 and Zech. 12:10), the Hebrews failed to accept these phenomena when they transpired before their eyes. Modern Christians are viewing the Bible "out of focus" when they regard the second coming of Christ as too extraordinary to be true. Thus did the first-century Hebrews regarding his first advent.

Meaning of His Coming

Admittedly, the second coming of Christ has meant different things to different people. There is sufficient play and flexibility of terminology in the Scriptures to necessitate a careful sifting of the evidence in seeking true meaning.

It is essentially a *parousia*. This Greek term means "presence, the presence of one coming, hence the coming, arrival, advent." Some interpreters siphon off "the advent" aspect of this word compounded of the preposition "by" or "with" and the verb "to be."

To some the term is synonymous with the expression "the

day of the Lord" (cf. 2 Peter 3:12). Yet the church fathers used it with an adjective and called it the second coming. In Matthew 24:3 the *parousia* clearly refers to "thy coming" (i.e. of Jesus Christ).

1. Some construe the *parousia* to have been realized with the coming of the Spirit on the day of Pentecost. They identify Christ and the Holy Spirit absolutely. Others maintain that it will be the coming of a general spirit of good will throughout the earth.

2. In John 14:3 Jesus said, "If I go and prepare a place for you, I come again, and will receive you unto myself; that where I am, there ye may be also" (ASV). Some contend that Jesus' words, "I come again," refer to his coming to each believer at the time of death.

3. A spiritualization of the second advent is achieved when men regard it as being fulfilled by the Lord's coming in great sweeping revivals. Every profound spiritual awakening is accompanied by the presence *(parousia)* of the Lord. Such visitations of purging, judgment, and improving of human welfare constitute the second advent of the Lord, according to this interpretation. *Revivalism and Social Reform* by Timothy L. Smith points up by implication the ultimate effect envisioned here.

4. The personal, bodily, visible return of Christ is the intent of the words directed to the disciples at the ascension of Christ. "Ye men of Galilee, why stand ye looking into heaven? this Jesus, who was received up from you into heaven, shall so come in like manner as ye beheld him going into heaven" (Acts 1:11, ASV). "This same Jesus" means personally. "Shall so come in like manner" means visibly. "As ye beheld him going into heaven" means bodily. They saw the Lord as he departed from them on the wings of a cloud; this set the pattern for the manner of his return.

An element of truth may be resident in each of the above

theories. The last is foremost. It appears to be primary in the teachings of both the Lord and the apostles.

Relevance of the Second Coming

Christian doctrines have practical value. Few Bible truths are intended as only luscious morsels to delight the doctrinal palate.

The second coming of Christ inspires men toward purity. "Every one that hath this hope set on him purifieth himself, even as he is pure" (1 John 3:3, ASV). "This hope" refers to the manifestation or appearance of Christ referred to in the preceding verse where John had just said that "we shall be like him; for we shall see him even as he is." Jesus may return at any time (or our death may occur immediately). No one knows the day nor the hour, save God the Father (Matt. 24:36). The fact that his coming could happen at any moment should incite every follower to live a pure life.

This hope should also incite Christians to set less value on the things of this present life and more upon the kingdom of God. "Seeing that these things [the physical universe, the earth on which we live] are thus all to be dissolved, what manner of persons ought ye to be in all holy living and godliness, looking for and earnestly desiring the coming of the day of God" (2 Peter 3:11-12, ASV). New heavens and a new earth will replace the old at the coming of Christ.

The Christian cannot afford to let his concern for investments in the present world overshadow his interest in the invisible, everlasting kingdom of Christ. The day of the Lord will reveal the values which we have sought and cherished. His return will be accompanied by "fire." At that time it will become evident immediately whether we have built with hay, wood, stubble, gold, or precious stone. "Every man's work shall be made manifest: . . . and the fire shall try every man's work of what sort it is" (1 Cor. 3:13).

Remaining in the Scriptural Orbit

It is axiomatic that scholars, preachers, and lay Christians often go off at a tangent when dealing with the second coming of Christ. Dozens of books on this subject in my library reflect practically all shades of emphasis, meaning, and interpretation. Equally good men espouse positions that are at opposite poles. Little wonder Christ enjoined caution.

The first extreme to be avoided is that of discounting the possibility of the second coming at all. The same Bible which depicts the first advent also warns about the second. "Knowing this first, that in the last days mockers shall come with mockery, walking after their own lusts, and saying, Where is the promise of his coming? for, from the day that the fathers fell asleep, all things continue as they were from the beginning of the creation" (2 Peter 3:3-4, ASV). Peter inveighs against those who lost faith in the reality of the return of Christ.

The Lord sharply rebukes those who are overly credulous on the subject. Recognizing that "many shall come in my name, saying, I am the Christ; and shall lead many astray," Jesus cautioned the disciples not to look upon every dramatic personality stalking across the stage of human history as the Messiah (Matt. 24:5, ASV). One pastor prior to the outbreak of World War II preached a sermon on the subject, "Thirty-one reasons why Mussolini is the Antichrist." The Jews in the days of early Christianity themselves went after Bar-Kochba as the Messiah in hopes of restored nationalism. Gullible voters have attributed messianic qualities to "promising" politicians and national leaders who keep a country's economic machinery well oiled.

It is necessary to distinguish between "imminent" and "immediate" return. The second coming of Christ is imminent in the sense that it could take place at any moment. There never has been a time when God could not have sent his Son back into the world to consummate what he began. However, the apostles and early Christians for a while assumed that the second coming must be immediate.

Members of the church at Thessalonica were so sure that the Lord was about to come that they gave up their jobs, ceased working, and started walking about, gazing into the heavens to see who could be first to spot the Lord as he started back to earth. They became "pious loafers" (cf. 1 Thess: 5:10-12, ASV).

We smile at these first-century Christians who became impractical in their reaction to the hope of the Lord's return, but what about the American Colony in the city of Jerusalem toward the end of the nineteenth century? These sincere, and in many cases brilliant, friends would go out to the Mount of Olives by night to wait for the Lord's return. They justified their action by the words, "His feet shall stand in that day upon the mount of Olives, which is before Jerusalem on the east" (Zech. 14:4, ASV). One saintly lady would take a cup of cold water ready to present it to the Lord "in the name of a disciple" upon his arrival.

Dr. Clovis G. Chappell in his *Sermons from Revelation* points out that:

Since the early saints believed in the immediate and visible return of Jesus, it is not a matter of wonder that many earnest and devout men and women have held to this faith through the centuries. There are those who believe it joyfully today. There are whole sects to which it is fundamental. A dozen years ago there was a certain slogan that one of these sects spread over billboards, shouted over radio, blazoned to the world in paid advertisements. It ran like this, "Millions now living will never die." It was a rather daring assertion, seeing that it could be so easily disproved. . . . A leading laundry, which had more humor than reverence, adopted the slogan as its own, making it read in this fashion: "We do the dyeing for the millions now living."[1]

---

[1](Nashville: Abingdon-Cokesbury Press, 1943), p. 206.

Elusive, Fascinating Facets

It is easy to become overly engrossed in the details associated with the second coming as well as some of the figurative language.

Some insist that Paul's reference to our being caught up "to meet the Lord in the air" (1 Thess. 4:17, ASV) is not to be taken literally. Others aver with equal enthusiasm that this is "the rapture" whereby the Lord will lift out of the world his followers just prior to "the great tribulation." The believers will remain in the air with the Lord until the tribulation is over and then descend with the Lord and reign with him a thousand years. Others maintain that "unconsecrated" Christians will remain on the earth for the duration of the tribulation and be purged by the time of the last trumpet.

Then, some interpret Daniel 9:27 to mean that this tribulation will last seven years (a year for each day). The last half of the verse means that in the middle of the tribulation (after three and one-half years) all religious influence will cease—"he shall cause the sacrifice and the oblation to cease and upon the wing of abominations shall come one that maketh desolate; and even unto the full end, and that determined, shall wrath be poured out upon the desolate" (ASV). Paul says in 2 Thessalonians 2:7-8 that this "mystery of lawlessness doth already work: only there is one that restraineth now, until he be taken out of the way" (ASV). The one that restraineth is thought by these interpreters to refer to the Holy Spirit. He will be taken out of the world after the first three and one-half years of the tribulation, leaving the wicked members of the human race in the world for three and one-half years longer to suffer the rule of Satan when all hell will be let loose. Meanwhile, Christians have been caught up with the Lord in the air until the end of the tribulation, it is believed.

At this point perhaps a word about the millennium becomes appropriate. The word "millennium" does not occur as such

REVELATION'S CONSUMMATION

in the Bible. The expression "a thousand years," for which the Latin word is "millennium," is found in only one chapter of the Bible, and that is Revelation 20. The expression "thousand years" does occur, however, in this chapter some six times. Many scholars recoil from the practice of building a theory around an expression found in only one chapter of the Bible and that in the most figurative book of the Bible.

A premillenialist believes that the world will continue to deteriorate morally and spiritually until Christ comes in order to save the human race. He will then reign on the earth with Christians for one thousand years (perhaps setting up headquarters in Palestine from which his kingdom will be managed, depending on how literal is the interpretation).

A postmillennialist believes that through the preaching of the gospel and the working of the Holy Spirit the world will become increasingly better until there will eventually be a thousand years of peace, righteousness, and prosperity for all humanity. At the end of this time Christ will return.

Others, apparently repelled by any form of "millennialism," move in the direction of amillennialism, or no millennium at all. They see only a figurative value to most dispensational terminology and let it go at that.

The Jewish scholar, Joseph Klausner, contends that Paul drew his ideas about "the last trumpet" from both Jerusalem and Babylon Talmud passages where it is used to call the exiles (Jews of the Diaspora) as well as to signal the resurrection of the dead.[2] He berates Paul for linking the last trumpet with the *parousia* and accuses him of accommodating Hebrew dispensationalism to his disappointment of Christ's not returning soon (1 Thess. 4:16).

These are intriguing facets of Bible teaching, and one could spend a lifetime studying them. Having read many volumes on the subject and while subscribing only to the basic aspects

---

[2] *Miyeshu ad Paulus*, (Tel-Aviv, Israel: Maida', 1940), II, 224-25.

of premillennialism, I attach only marginal importance thereto. Many Christians and preachers become so preoccupied with these matters, regardless of the view espoused, that they often neglect the one thing that the Lord would have them do, namely, "make disciples of all the nations."

Christ is coming, but before or after what is not as important as the fact itself. Winsome Christians have been on opposite sides of the question. But any man will be more winsome if he refuses to let such a subject or any detail thereof overshadow his emphasis on character growth, Christlike love, and undiminishing service. The fact that great soul-winners and fruitful Christians can espouse different views of the Lord's return proves that what a man believes about "millennialism" is not a chief determinant of his effectiveness as a servant of God. Even if we knew beyond any doubt, which we certainly do not, that Christ would return to this earth bodily by tomorrow night at 6:00 P.M., we should spend our time doing one thing, namely, evangelizing lost men who are on the verge of being projected into eternity without Christ.

This truth is potent but it must be dealt with temperately. For example, there was

a band of religious enthusiasts in England under the Commonwealth, who expected the personal appearance of Jesus Christ to found with their armed assistance a new or fifth monarchy—its predecessors being the Babylonian, Persian Greek, and Roman monarchies supposed to be referred to in *Daniel ii.* They were particularly strong in the Cromwellian army, and in 1657 a number of them under Venner attempted an insurrection in London, calling upon the godly to introduce the reign of Christ and expel all carnal sovereignties. Cromwell got wind of the affair and clapped the ringleaders into gaol. In 1661 Venner made another rising, and the fanatic and sixteen of his accomplices were executed.[3]

---

[3]E. Royston Pike, *Encyclopaedia of Religion and Religions* (London: George Allen & Unwin, 1952), p. 153.

On the other hand, today rationalism all but snuffs out justifiable interest in the doctrine of the second coming. Is it likely that we are placing ourselves in the position of the Jews who repudiated the first coming of Christ?

Scientists are now speaking openly about a possible cataclysmic consummation of the universe. Anything could happen, according to men of physics and astronomy. One scientist on the west coast recently referred to the theory of an "exploding universe" and described how huge stars and planets larger than our own come into certain realms of space only to disappear as apparent "sparks" in a gigantic explosion. But amazingly enough, other planets come in to take their place. From where is not known. Science has no explanation for their appearance or existence. This is one we possibly should "refer to our clergymen," said the scientist.

Can modern theologians afford to become so preoccupied with the processes of temporality that when the scientist, of all men, would cue him in he forgets his lines? "That one supreme, divine event toward which all creation moves" is a part of the theologian's message. It should well be a part of the prayer of us all—"Even so, come, Lord Jesus" (Rev. 22:20).

Biographical Sketches

Angel Martinez

Angel Martinez is a Southern Baptist evangelist who was born in San Antonio, Texas, of Latin-American parents. He is a graduate of Baylor University and Southern Baptist Theological Seminary. In addition, he has completed more than two years' study on a law degree. Mr. Martinez is married and has two children. He makes his home in Fort Smith, Arkansas.

Paul S. James

Paul S. James is director of Southern Baptist work in metropolitan New York. Until recently, he also served as pastor of the Manhattan Baptist Church in New York City. Dr. James is a graduate of Wheaton College and Southern Baptist Theological Seminary. He was pastor of the Second Baptist Church in Auburn, New York, and Tabernacle Baptist Church in Atlanta, Georgia, before going to New York. Dr. James is married and has three children.

Clyde T. Francisco

Clyde T. Francisco is John R. Sampey Professor of Old Testament Interpretation at Southern Baptist Theological

Seminary in Louisville, Kentucky. He is a graduate of the University of Richmond and Southern Seminary. In addition, he has done graduate work at a number of other schools. Dr. Francisco is married and has two children. He is the author of two books.

Robert Greene Lee

Robert Greene Lee is pastor emeritus of Bellevue Baptist Church, Memphis, Tennessee. A native of South Carolina, Dr. Lee is a graduate of Furman University and Chicago Law School. He held pastorates in South Carolina and Louisiana prior to going to Bellevue. Dr. Lee has served three terms as president of the Southern Baptist Convention. He is the author of numerous books and is well known for his sermon entitled "Pay-Day—Someday."

Carl F. H. Henry

Carl F. H. Henry is editor of *Christianity Today*. He is a graduate of Wheaton College, Northern Baptist Theological Seminary, and Boston University. In addition, he has done graduate work at several other schools. Dr. Henry has been professor of theology at Northern Seminary and Fuller Theological Seminary. He is the author of numerous books. Dr. Henry is married and has two children. He resides in Arlington, Virginia, while his office and church membership are in Washington, D. C.

J. D. Grey

J. D. Grey is pastor of the First Baptist Church in New Orleans, Louisiana. A native of Kentucky, Dr. Grey is a graduate of Union University and Southwestern Baptist Theological Seminary. Dr. Grey has served two terms as president of the Southern Baptist Convention. He has traveled extensively. Dr. Grey is married and has twin daughters.

Herschel H. Hobbs

Herschel H. Hobbs is pastor of the First Baptist Church, Oklahoma City, Oklahoma. A native of Alabama, Dr. Hobbs is a graduate of Howard College and Southern Baptist Theological Seminary. He held pastorates in Alabama, Indiana, Kentucky, and Louisiana prior to going to Oklahoma City. He serves as speaker for the Baptist Hour, a weekly radio program. Dr. Hobbs has traveled extensively. He is the author of numerous books. Dr. Hobbs is married and has one son.

L. Nelson Bell

L. Nelson Bell is executive editor of *Christianity Today*. A native of Virginia, Dr. Bell is a graduate of Washington and Lee University and Medical College of Virginia. He served for twenty-five years as a chief surgeon in China under the Board of World Missions, Presbyterian Church in the United States. Another fifteen years were spent in the practice of surgery in Asheville, North Carolina. Dr. Bell has traveled extensively.

H. Leo Eddleman

H. Leo Eddleman is president of New Orleans Baptist Theological Seminary. He is a native of Mississippi and a graduate of Mississippi College and Southern Baptist Theological Seminary. Before coming to New Orleans Seminary, Dr. Eddleman held pastorates in Kentucky, taught at Baptist Bible Institute and Southern Seminary, served as a missionary in the Middle East, and served as president of Georgetown College. Dr. Eddleman is married and has two daughters.